SPEAK UP!

A PERSONAL STORIES PROJECT

A Sub/Urban Justice Publication

ACKNOWLEDGEMENTS

Brought to you by the Speak Up! Team –

Blen Girum, Hannah Birnbaum, Jenna Spencer, Kristen Jones, and Chris Messinger.

Thanks to Boston Mobilization and Sub/Urban Justice for their continued support.

Additional thanks to:

Vanessa Abanu	Ekua Holmes	Lisa Owens
Leila Alciere	Dave Jenkins	Riva Pearson
Donna Bivens	Jack Kahn	Cynthia Peters
Julian Braxton	Jonathon Kozol	Zoe Peters
Steve Clem	Paul Kuttner	Eli Plenk
Mariel Cohn	Adam Machson-Carter	Rebecca Price
Ted Cullinane	Jesse McGleughlin	Tom Rust
Tracy Curtin	Paul Marcus	Steven Tejada
Ty DePass	Pat Maher	William Poff-Webster
Patti DeRosa	Susan Mayer	Dr. Jim Spencer
Jenny Ding	Dr. Peggy McIntosh	Dr. Beverly Daniel Tatum
Heather Flewelling	Cara McKenna	Gabrielle Thal-Pruzan
Bill Gardiner	Annery Miranda	Tara Venkatraman
James Greenwood	Sue Naimark	Symone Williams
Meck Groot	Jolie Olivetti	Tim Wise
Donna Halper	Akinyi Opeyo	Howard Zinn

and the numerous folks we've unintentionally omitted and the countless role models who have inspired and supported us along the way.

This book is dedicated to the students who fill our independent schools across New England, and who continue to challenge systems of oppression everywhere.

"Hope is believing despite the evidence, and then watching the evidence change."

– Jim Wallis

FOREWORD

for Educators

When I first heard about the Speak Up! Project from Sub/Urban Justice, I knew immediately that it would be helpful on many levels: helpful to the young people who would tell their stories, helpful to the educators who would read them, and helpful to the institutions that could use the stories as catalysts for reflection and transformation.

Every school has an overt curriculum, best understood as all of the planned experiences that students have at school, and what has come to be called a hidden curriculum, which consists of everything unintended that students experience and learn at school. The stories you will read in this book spring from the hidden curriculum, for every student in these pages has learned something painful and indelible that no one at the school could possibly have intended. The stories cover a wide range of topics: racism, homophobia, religious discrimination, and feelings of being marginalized and silenced. These stories break the silence and I am grateful that so many young people had the courage to share their truth.

When I first became a full-time independent school administrator in the early 1980s, the great majority of independent schools were overwhelmingly white in terms of students and faculty, but had a sprinkling of students of color. The prevailing attitude, usually hiding just below the surface, was that 1) we were doing these students a great service, 2) they were lucky to be at our schools and 3) they should be grateful for the opportunity. We never said these things out loud, but we loved it when the students and their families said them. We almost never thought about the social, emotional, and spiritual price "those students" were paying simply by coming to "our schools" day in and day out. We rarely asked them about what it was really like to be one of the few folks of color in the school. Not only did we not ask them to tell us their stories, we made it clear in subtle, unspoken ways that we really did not want to hear anything that might challenge our comfortable and comforting assumptions. I have since spoken to many colleagues of color who went through our schools in those days and they all remember a lot of pain mixed in with the benefits.

It is encouraging that over the last 20 years our schools have made progress in acknowledging the problems and in becoming more truly multicultural institutions. The challenge is that—as these stories make clear—there is still a lot of work to be done. Everywhere. Neither the students nor the schools are identified here because there is a universality to the experiences of students who represent difference from the "norms" in our schools, and the kinds of experiences described here could happen—and probably have happened—at any school. No one should be saying, "Well, that couldn't happen here." Denial is not an option. You cannot start to change your hidden curriculum if you are not willing to uncover it.

Let me be clear to the educators reading this book – just reading the stories is not enough; just reading the stories and feeling sad or bad or guilty is not enough. You have to do something with the knowledge and insights these stories give you. You need to commit to action. By your actions you will honor the courage and honesty of these students. But don't forget, these students don't just have insights into what isn't working - they are also the experts in what will work and what has worked for them. Let's be sure to include our most important resource in the conversation!

Here's our assignment: work on ourselves and our institutions so that, starting tomorrow and progressing steadily, our schools will be better places for students and adults who embody difference from the traditional norms. Our schools must strive to realize the goal of having all students and adults feel, as a student of color once put it, "unselfconsciously included."

Steve Clem

Executive Director

Association of Independent Schools in New England (AISNE)

TABLE OF CONTENTS

Foreword...2
Introduction 6
      How to Use this Book..7
      Who We Are 8
      Visual Artist Statements 10
What Is Racism? 12
Race, Racism, and Racial Prejudice 16
      40 Acres and a Mule..17
      Whiteness..20
Identity and Interpersonal Racism..24
      Good Hair Day...26
      The Real Deal 29
      Are *You* Mexican? 32
      The Importance of Identity 33
Institutional Racism 37
      The *Liberal* Institution..39
      It's More Than Students..41
Ideological Racism 44
      Voting on Your Values...45
      Separation...48
      Who's a Terrorist?...49
Internalized Racism..52
      Hair..53
      Shame 55
      Better Than? 58
      Diversity Is Bullsh*t..60
A Closer Look: Special Treatment or Safe Space? 62
      Separate. But Equal? 63
      Our Safe Space 64
Identities and Intersections 67
      Untitled 68
      The Other F Word 70
      Part of Your World 71
      Taught to Kill 73
Vision...76
Strategies/Actions/Resources 80
      Responsibility..82
      Hope..83
      Lunch Time 89
Conclusion 105
Citations 106
School Contacts 107

I am an invisible man. I am a man of substance, of flesh and bone, fiber and liquids - and I might even be said to possess a mind. I am invisible, understand, simply because people refuse to see me.
—Ralph Ellison

SPEAK UP! AN INTRODUCTION

Race and racism are very complex concepts. While race has no biological significance, it has somehow become omnipresent in our lives and culture. Furthermore, while everyone has an opinion, we are socialized not to talk about race! We are encouraged to pretend to be color blind, but deep down we know that is impossible. White people who talk openly about race are stared at with confusion and find their opinions negated. People of color who talk openly about race are glared at and accused of 'playing the race card.'

Considering the social implications of discussing race, why would we, a group of teens from distinguished independent schools in New England, want to speak up about this issue? Why would we want to share our experiences and the experiences of other teens with the larger community? Why would we take the initiative and the time to pull together a book of stories?

Like many of you reading this, we feel responsible for our school, our community, and the world at large. We met each other in the summer of 2008 through the Sub/Urban Justice Summer program (www.suburbanjustice.org). Sub/Urban Justice supports young people to develop leadership and community organizing skills in order to transform their urban and suburban communities into places of justice and equity. We identified racism as the most pressing problem in our schools, and formed a group to counteract it. Sub/Urban Justice helped us develop the skills to take action on this complex and significant issue.

In this book, you will read stories from an array of independent school students. While they all share a similar educational background, the authors of these stories represent a range of racial, ethnic, and cultural identities. As you read their stories, you will experience a variety of opinions and feelings about race that range from anger and guilt to sadness and hope. We hope that through this diversity of experiences, you will be able to identify with one or more of these students' stories, and be inspired to take action against racism.

HOW TO USE THIS BOOK

This book is a compilation of true stories of real students at New England independent private schools in the past few years. It is not a workbook, reader, or manual. It is an opportunity, a resource, and a guide. We believe that talking about something as complicated as race and racism requires clear communication and a shared language. If we do not understand each other – or if we are using the same words to mean different things – we will not have a productive conversation. This starts by defining racism and offering other definitions of key terms periodically used throughout. We also include inspiring and challenging quotations from prominent thinkers and occasional visual images.

Please use this book in any way you see fit. Personal stories are critical to understanding different perspectives, but there are many other ways to think about complex issues. There are also questions and activities at the end of each story - but do not feel pressured to complete them right away. Many of these stories call for quiet reflection. When you're ready, feel free to engage with the included questions with a partner or by yourself and begin a dialogue. We also encourage readers to write a response and submit it to the Speak Up! Project at www.speakupstories. org. Our suggestions are just that – suggestions. Use this book in whatever way suits you best. It's YOURS!

Finally, the authors and the schools in this book are anonymous. School names and any other information that may help identify specific schools have been removed. We chose this approach because racism exists everywhere. We are not trying to spotlight a school or a person, nor are we suggesting there is only one way to address issues of racism. This book is full of experiences, not suggestions. At its heart is a very powerful message: you can do something about these problems. You, reading this right now, can work against racism. And more than that, we believe that you and your peers know what needs to be done to make your school a better place. When you stop to think about it – that's pretty powerful.

WHO WE ARE

"I believe the Speak Up! Project has a strong potential to play a vital role in academic discourse within our schools. This is an opportunity to empower students to freely express themselves on a systemic oppression such as racism." **Blen Girum** (Cambridge School of Weston '09) worked with the Sub/Urban Justice Summer Program (SJS '08) as an active participant. Throughout her senior year she worked tirelessly to gather stories and edit the Anthology. As a first year at Cornell, Blen continued to stay involved, working over her winter break to finalize the Speak Up! Anthology.

"Many people living on the East Coast always talk about how racist the south is, while denying the racism that exists in their own backyards. The Speak Up! Project is so important, because it draws attention to the discrimination that exists all across the United States. Nobody can deny someone else's personal story." **Jenna Spencer** participated in the Sub/Urban Justice Program in 2008 for six weeks to further enhance her interest and knowledge of social justice issues. She has attended a small New England private school since her freshman year of high school and will be graduating with the class of 2010.

"Through using personal stories, I believe that people will understand that racism still exists and more importantly it still exists in our own communities. Our goal is not to condemn others, but to give a voice and story to those who are not heard. Through these stories, I wish to bring

education and reflection to my own community." **Hannah Birnbaum** (Nobles and Greenough '10) participated in SJS '08, and returned in '09 as a Youth Community Leader. During her senior year ('09-'10), Hannah conducted a series of workshops at local independent schools.

"What I find most compelling about this project is the way in which these students have chosen to tackle such a huge problem like racism – with the use of personal stories. We hope that these personal stories will open up dialogue about racism between students, administrators, and parents so that we can make conscious steps together toward ending racism." **Kristen Jones** (Harvard '10) worked with the Sub/Urban Justice Summer Program (SJS '08, SJS '09) as a full-time staffer, and continued as the primary program staffer for the Speak Up! Project. She is also a graduate from an independent school in her home state of Louisiana.

Do: Read this cover to cover; Skip around; Talk about it with your friends;

Don't: Forget the strategies section; Hesitate to contact us for support;

Do: Try out the Activities; Pause after each story; Answer questions; Invite Speak Up! to your school; Remember YOU can make a difference.

"The Speak Up! Project is so powerful because it relies on story and lived experience as a teaching tool. It's an example of engaged students making their curriculum more responsive - and tackling the issue that is most impacting them in a tangible way. I wish Speak Up! had been available when I was a student." **Chris Messinger** is the Executive Director of Boston Mobilization, a youth empowerment non-profit operating in the Greater Boston area for the past three decades. He is also the proud graduate of two fine Massachusetts independent schools.

VISUAL ARTISTS STATEMENTS

While the story authors are anonymous, the visual artists wanted the opportunity to explain their art. Below are their statements – a listing of the pages their art appears on follows each statement.

These pieces of art are part of my "altered book" project. I used an important resource *The Negro In America: A Bibliography* as the template for my art. I wanted to make a statement about race, identity, and the struggle for freedom by complementing the bibliography with images creating a powerful statement. For example, I used many images of a silhouette of a person with her arms spread wide. I used quotes by Ralph Ellison, Stokely Carmichael, Martin Luther King Jr., Toni Morrison, and Angela Davis; great thinkers and activists on race and racism in the United States.

The assembled images range from slave ships and silhouettes to word charts and dictionary definitions of identity and racism. Through my " altered book" I sought to illuminate an ignored history and render people "visible." I hope that this art will encourage people to think deeply about racism, oppression, and the struggle for liberation.

– Jesse McGleughlin

Our grandfathers had to run, run, run. My generation's out of breath. We ain't running no more
Stokely Carmichael

Jesse's art appears on pages 5, 14, 19, 23, 31, 43, 51, 57, 59, 72 and 79

VISUAL ARTISTS STATEMENTS

Each one of the pieces I have in this book is meant to complicate our approach to race in American History. History is messy: it is chaotic and nuanced and contradictory. However, often our education system ignores the beautiful complexity of our history. The symbols I used are meant to be slightly jarring: they are familiar images used in unfamiliar ways. I hope my pieces prompt questions rather than give answers and I hope they inspire readers to see the importance of critical engagement with the past. In the infinitely wise words of Maya Angelou: "History, despite its wrenching pain, cannot be unlived, but if faced with courage, need not be lived again."

– Eli Plenk

Eli's art appears on pages 90, 101 and 104

WHAT IS RACISM?

When most people use the word "racism," they are usually referring to an exchange between two (or sometimes more) people - Rosa Parks and a bus driver; a slur shouted in the heat of the moment; a racial joke told at someone's expense. But this simple definition is incomplete. If we define racism as only between two people, how then do we account for schools that historically denied admission to certain racial groups, or the classic experiment that showed that young children of color preferred playing with white dolls (described later in this book), or the ways in which the media today influences our thoughts and perceptions?

As we gathered these stories from our classmates, friends, and peers at some of the 250 independent schools in New England, it became clear that racism in private schools has many different faces. Racism is sometimes present in our interpersonal interactions, but it is also present in our private thoughts, in our educational institutions and the media that surrounds us. Together, these different aspects of racism make up a "system" - with all of the parts combining to keep racism alive and functioning in our world.

In this book, we identify four interrelated parts of this system and separate them into four areas, which we call "The Four I's." Each of these "I's" represents a different area of our lives, from our **Internalized** beliefs and convictions to our **Interpersonal** exchanges, to our life in **Institutions**, to the **Ideology** that shapes what we think and do.

Another way to think about **Ideology** is culture. We have separated the stories into different chapters to help highlight each of these different aspects of racism, but ask you to remember that they are functioning as part of a whole system. We use these "I's" as a way to help us process the complexity and dynamic nature of racism in our lives.

We think of "**The Four I's**" with the following metaphor. First, imagine a person. They have their own thoughts and feelings, beliefs and prejudices, hopes and dreams, which are held **Internally**. This person goes through life and interacts with other people – their internal self interacts **Interpersonally** with other individuals.

As they travel through the world, they are also constantly interacting with **Institutions** and **Systems**. In this case, they are within the **Institution** of a school, within the **System** of education.

These **Internal** beliefs and **Interpersonal** and **Institutional** interactions are all shaped by the **Ideology**, the system of beliefs, the Culture we live in. Our metaphorical person sees the world through a set of values, norms and standards that allow them to judge what is wrong or right, what is strange or normal, and what is good or bad. Their personal ideology is influenced by both conscious and subconscious messages present in many aspects of our everyday lives – from our families and schools to our media and institutions of faith.

Together, these four "I's" shape every facet of our lives and experiences – and together they make up the system of racism. We'll look at each of them more closely through personal stories. As you can imagine, these four aspects of racism are tightly connected. For example, we are each attached to various **institutions** that both rely on and shape the **ideological** and cultural perspectives of our world. The **institutions** we are involved with often give power to our **interpersonal** interactions. We cannot have an **interpersonal** interaction without relying on our **internalized** perspectives. And all of us consume media and have been raised with **ideological** and **cultural** perspectives.

What can we do about racism?

Because many people think of racism as simply interpersonal exchanges, most people only think of interpersonal strategies. But, we have a different strategy. Our goal is to address the entire system of racism, which includes all four levels. Our first step? Recruiting you to work with us to take action. Racism is a system - it will require many groups of us working together to fully change it. We have some ideas about how to do this, but we are not the experts on your school. We think you know what is best for your school's community and have some great ideas about how to change your school for the better. In the Strategies section you'll find some skills and suggestions from other students about how to turn your good ideas into real change. We think that students - especially the students most impacted by racism - understand what needs to be done to meet their basic needs, and have a critical responsibility to demand what they want.

Finally, race and racism are evolving every day. Because of the ever-changing nature of race and racism, we must develop new strategies to challenge racial oppression. No longer is racism legally sanctioned in the areas of jobs or housing or education. Today, we are living in a world with more covert instances of racism. For example, individuals with African-American sounding names have diminished chances of being hired (See Sidebar, p. 15). How can we challenge this kind of racism?

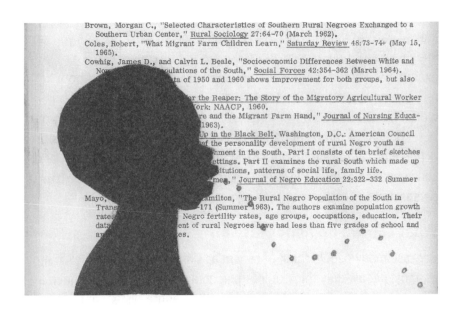

Brown, Morgan C., "Selected Characteristics of Southern Rural Negroes Exchanged to a Southern Urban Center," Rural Sociology 27:64-70 (March 1962).
Coles, Robert, "What Migrant Farm Children Learn," Saturday Review 48:73-74+ (May 15, 1965).
Cowhig, James D., and Calvin L. Beale, "Socioeconomic Differences Between White and No... ...ulations of the South," Social Forces 42:354-362 (March 1964). ...ta of 1950 and 1960 shows improvement for both groups, but also

...r the Reaper: The Story of the Migratory Agricultural Worker ...ork: NAACP, 1960. ...re and the Migrant Farm Hand," Journal of Nursing Educa- ...1963). ...p in the Black Belt. Washington, D.C.: American Council ...f the personality development of rural Negro youth as ...hment in the South. Part I consists of ten brief sketches ...ettings. Part II examines the rural South which made up ...itutions, patterns of social life, family life. ...me," Journal of Negro Education 22:322-332 (Summer

Mayo, ...amilton, "The Rural Negro Population of the South in Trans... ...171 (Summer 1963). The authors examine population growth rates ... Negro fertility rates, age groups, occupations, education. Their data ...ent of rural Negroes have had less than five grades of school and a... ...es.

What's in a Name?

Researchers at the University of Chicago and MIT submitted 5,000 nearly identical resumes to 1,250 advertisers seeking administrative and sales help. The catch? Half of the resumes had the most common white names according to birth records (Brendan, Gregg, Emily and Anne) while the other half used the most common African-American names (Tamika, Aisha, Rasheed and Tyrone). The results? The "white" applicants received one response--a call, letter or e-mail--for every 10 resumes mailed, while African-Americans with equal credentials received one response for every 15 resumes. The racial gap was uniform across occupation, industry and employer size. There were no significant differences between the rates at which men and women were contacted. What accounts for this discrepancy?

MIT Researcher Sendhil Mullainathan has the following response, "It doesn't seem like the problem is that they're sitting there going, 'Well, I really don't want Tamika here.' The problem seems to be that they read through hundreds of resumes very fast and try to form an impression of the person from the resume. And subconsciously, if you see the name Tamika it's going to bleed into your overall impression, it's going to cue all the negative stereotypes you might have implicitly ...of African-Americans, and I think that's hard to challenge."

RACE, RACISM, AND RACIAL PREJUDICE

The following chapter includes stories and poems that explore one element at the heart of racism - prejudice. A prejudice [definition: pre-conceived judgment or opinion] does not independently have a positive or negative connotation. It is only a pre-judgment. But how are these prejudgments used? Psychologist Gordon Allport, who conducted in-depth and ground-breaking research on the creation and development of prejudice in young people, has said: "Prejudgments become prejudices only if they are not reversible when exposed to new knowledge." This book is an opportunity to gain new knowledge about the real experiences of students around race and racism. Even if we are trained to prejudge those around us, these stories are an opportunity to see the world through a different lens.

[race]: a social construction used to characterize groups of people.

[skin privilege]: the institutional and interpersonal advantages one receives solely because of his or her skin tone.

[culture]: the set of shared attitudes, values, goals, and practices that characterizes an institution or organization.

[systemic oppression]: institutional systems in place to subordinate a group of people by force, authority, or societal norms.

[white privilege]: the institutional advantages – socially, politically, financially, and culturally – people receive solely because they are perceived as white.

" ** *Racism is nothing more or less than white privilege, white power, and white violence.* **"

– Manning Marable, 1997

40 ACRES AND A MULE

Seemed more like curse than blessin
Felt like confessin wit no guilt
Cause of the place race built
If you got a black face than its guilt by association
Goin from elation to deflation
Treated like fuck them we can replace them
Beat them even mace them
And they say this is a great nation?
They used to think we only 3/5 gods creation
Am I the only one to find this odd?
We're not even a whole person but still 90 percent of little Brad's ipod
Cause he loves the struggle and how we depict it
He can't handle the whole truth so we give him a snippet
Of what we went through gotta go through jus to get to
What u got cause your hairs blonde and your eyes blue
I got all this anger built up cause I finally see the truth
That I gotta be 5 times better than you
So I don't get looked passed at an interview
Or be placed under you
So we look to sports rappin or trappin
As our only avenue to get a view of Park Avenue
Where to get my 40 acres and a mule
I gotta entertain sum fool jus to get a back yard wit a pool
U sittin cool while I break my back jus to relax
Don't worry I know the truth even though society wants to skip facts
Forget wat u say wat u think of blacks
Ima keep my head held high cause I refuse to fall through the cracks
But why does society think so little of me
Instead of seeing me in a class that's AP
It would rather see me in a jumpsuit in juvie
And because I don't like to wear a collard shirt wit khakis

I'll rather wear a fitted cap wit Nikes
Does that make me different than yall
Why am I only recognized as the typical Negro that only dances
and plays ball
I've been tryna speak out but people don't listen when I call
So I'm forced to take it in my own hands and try to make the
prejudice fall

Questions: Please reflect on the piece you just read and answer the following questions.

❑ What are some of the examples of race-based prejudice exhibited in this piece?

❑ Who is responsible for creating these prejudices?

❑ Who is responsible for keeping them in place?

❑ Do you think public perceptions of young African American men as being in 'juvie' rather than AP classes has an impact on African American students at your school?

❑ What are some strategies you can think of to "make the prejudice fall"?

ACTIVITY Name five positive role models provided by the media in each of the following categories:

African Americans   Asian Americans   Indigenous Americans   European Americans

_____   _____   _____   _____

_____   _____   _____   _____

_____   _____   _____   _____

_____   _____   _____   _____

_____   _____   _____   _____

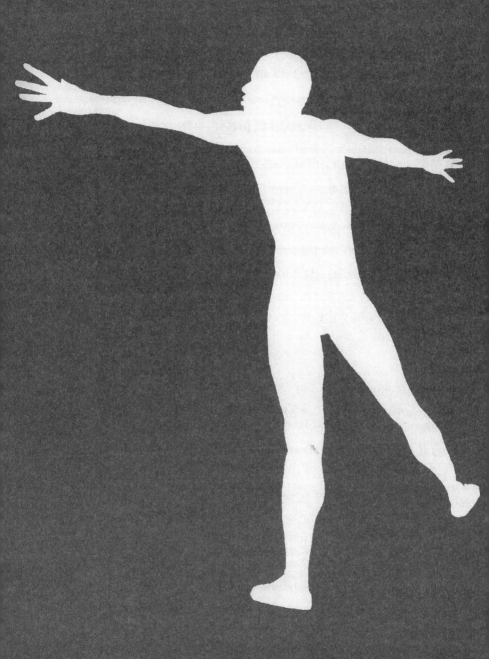

A Step Further: The author of this story says that s/he would have to "entertain sum fool jus to get a back yard wit a pool," which speaks to a common stereotype that black people can only be financially successful when entertaining. Do the role models that you've just brainstormed fit into commonly held stereotypes about these groups? If so, how?

WHITENESS

The police car rolled around the corner, lights flickering…red, blue… blue, red. Trapped in the spotlight, the hypnotizing sirens whirred before our eyes. My friend and I looked at each other; the expression in our eyes was easily exchangeable. Between our blue pupils and blonde hair, we questioned: "What should we do? Run?" But our consciences and "honest" upbringing taught us otherwise.

We reluctantly emerged from behind the brick edifice, walking dreadfully towards the menacing policeman. He peered at us from behind his tinted windowpane, sizing us up. And what do I think he saw?

Two kids…

Tan and blonde…

Blue-eyed…

Wealthy…

Educated, from the private school variety…

Christian, probably Protestant…

> " Speechless, anxious, and somewhat confused about the policeman's ignorance, I finally realized I was white. "

Just two kids caught in the wrong place at the wrong time…

He questioned us about our presence, but quickly drove away, believing everything we said. Speechless, anxious, and somewhat confused about the policeman's ignorance, I finally realized I was white.

From that moment on, I realized the meaning of whiteness, the meaning of privilege, the meaning of incessant advantages wherever I go. But from that moment on, I hated who I was. I hated the fact that everything was given to me, almost automatically—no questions asked. Based on my WASPy appearance, I have been deprived of the meaning of hard work; no matter how much I fail, I will always be picked up. Someone, by virtue of societal associations, will ensure that I don't fail—that I don't fail math class, that I don't get arrested, that I don't drop out of school. Due to my white background, I have a natural support system built into everything I do.

Yes, I am thankful. Yes, I should be thankful—I can do whatever I want. But really, I hate this support system, this constant assistance, this America. I hate it because I want to attribute my accomplishments to my own hard work, not my background, my inheritance, my family, my school. I hate it because I do work hard—I want to succeed…but my success will always be measured by my background. I really hate it because I am taking away opportunities from others. I hate it because I feel unfair, because I feel undeserving, because I want to give someone else a chance. I hate it all.

I wish I could have been someone else, someone who prevailed against the odds, someone with rich skin and a cultured background. I have none of this—my descendants came to America on the Mayflower, leaving me with an unpigmented, uncolored history. You could say I'm as American as it gets, but I'm really not...not at all.

America to me is something different—something unique or diverse. I am neither. America should be a melting pot of cultures and customs, yet I am always removed from this amalgamation of differences. Yes, I feel safe, I feel untouchable, but being white makes me guilty, makes me faulted, makes me embarrassed.

I really wish I weren't white. I hate it.

Questions: Please reflect on the piece you just read and answer the following questions.

❏ What are some of the privileges the author notes in this story?

❏ Where do these privileges come from?

❏ Why do these privileges upset the author?

❏ The author mentions a support 'system'. How is this system connected to the system of oppression the author described in the first story?

ACTIVITY List two things you like about your racial identity. List two things you dislike about your racial identity.

A Step Further: How can you use privileges associated with your race to help others or combat racism? How can you address feelings of guilt or shame attached to your race? Visit our 'Strategies' section for some helpful resources.

SECTION WRAP

The previous two stories highlighted both the positive and negative prejudices held by other people.

❏ What are some of the prejudices that others attribute to your race or ethnicity?

❏ Are they based in reality?

❏ Do they have a positive or negative impact? If you had a choice, would you keep or remove these prejudices?

❏ What are some prejudices you hold about your own race/ ethnicity? What are some prejudices you hold about other races or ethnicities?

A Step Further: The first author speaks about all the benefits of white privilege they are not entitled to, while the second author wishes they could have been someone who 'prevailed against the odds'. If you could choose to be either author for the rest of your life, which would you be?

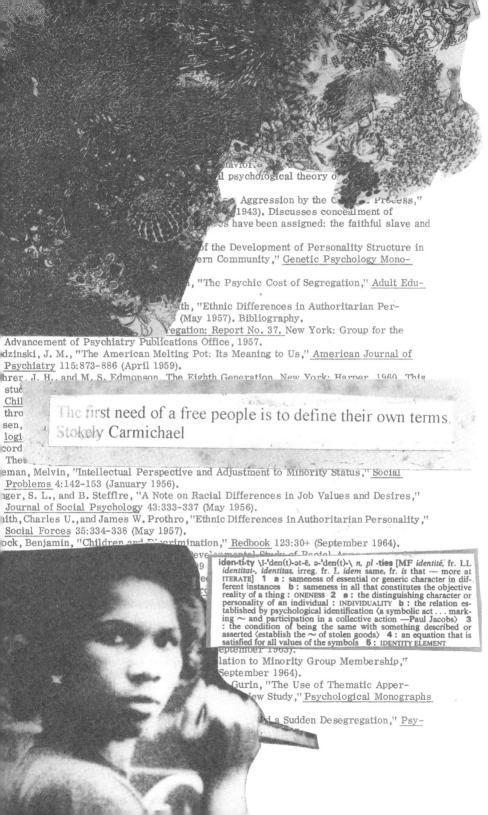

...havior...

...l psychological theory o...

...Aggression by the C...... Pr...ess," ...1943). Discusses concealment of ...s have been assigned: the faithful slave and

...f the Development of Personality Structure in ...ern Community," <u>Genetic Psychology Mono-</u>

..., "The Psychic Cost of Segregation," <u>Adult Edu-</u>

...th, "Ethnic Differences in Authoritarian Per- ...(May 1957). Bibliography.

...egation: <u>Report No. 37.</u> New York: Group for the Advancement of Psychiatry Publications Office, 1957.

...dzinski, J. M., "The American Melting Pot: Its Meaning to Us," <u>American Journal of Psychiatry</u> 115:873-886 (April 1959).

...hrer, J. H., and M. S. Edmonson, The Eighth Generation. New York: Harper, 1960. This stud...

Chil...
thro...
sen,...
logi...
cord...
The...

> The first need of a free people is to define their own terms.
> Stokely Carmichael

...eman, Melvin, "Intellectual Perspective and Adjustment to Minority Status," <u>Social Problems</u> 4:142-153 (January 1956).

...ger, S. L., and B. Stefflre, "A Note on Racial Differences in Job Values and Desires," <u>Journal of Social Psychology</u> 43:333-337 (May 1956).

...ith, Charles U., and James W. Prothro, "Ethnic Differences in Authoritarian Personality," <u>Social Forces</u> 35:334-338 (May 1957).

...ock, Benjamin, "Children and Discrimination," <u>Redbook</u> 123:30+ (September 1964).

...evelopmental Study of Racial Aw...

iden·ti·ty \ĭ-'den(t)-ət-ē, ə-'den(t)-\ *n, pl* **-ties** [MF *identité,* fr. LL *identitat-, identitas,* irreg. fr. *L idem* same, fr. *is* that — more at ITERATE] **1 a** : sameness of essential or generic character in different instances **b** : sameness in all that constitutes the objective reality of a thing : ONENESS **2 a** : the distinguishing character or personality of an individual : INDIVIDUALITY **b** : the relation established by psychological identification ⟨a symbolic act . . . marking ~ and participation in a collective action —Paul Jacobs⟩ **3** : the condition of being the same with something described or asserted ⟨establish the ~ of stolen goods⟩ **4** : an equation that is satisfied for all values of the symbols **5** : IDENTITY ELEMENT

...eptember 1965).

...lation to Minority Group Membership," ...September 1964).

...Gurin, "The Use of Thematic Apper- ...ew Study," <u>Psychological Monographs</u>

...d a Sudden Desegregation," <u>Psy-</u>

IDENTITY AND INTERPERSONAL RACISM

We mentioned the four "**I**'s" of racism in our introduction – **Interpersonal, Institutional, Ideological,** and **Internalized**. This chapter takes a closer look at **Interpersonal** racism, the most easily identifiable form of racism. This chapter also focuses on the ways in which our identities shape our interpersonal interactions. Identity is a critical component of our lives, giving us meaning and direction. We are children and grandchildren, siblings, friends, teammates, citizens of a nation and more. When our identities are devalued, we can feel isolated, disconnected, unsettled, and unable to act. However, when we strongly identify with our identities, we feel at home, comfortable – and sometimes willing to take risks. We are also occasionally empowered to act out in ways we otherwise would not.

When Rosa Parks refused to give up her seat on December 1, 1955, she, the white passengers, the bus driver, and the police all acted out their racial prejudgments from a place of identity. However, it is important to note that one side had the power of the law, the criminal justice system, history, and public custom behind them when acting in that moment. On the other hand, Rosa Parks had the power of people behind her – she was a part of a movement, part of a collective effort to address unequal treatment. Rosa Parks and the Civil Rights Movement used 'power with' to combat mainstream society's effort at 'power over'. Rosa Parks was not alone in her effort to challenge racism, and neither are you.

The following stories and poems revolve around those moments when one person engages another person using their own racially prejudiced beliefs. While each party has an equal opportunity to exert a racially prejudiced belief, pay attention to who has the power of systems and institutions behind them in each exchange.

[ethnicity]: of, or relating to, large groups of people classed according to common racial, national, tribal, religious, linguistic, or cultural origin or background

Race is an example of a social construction. We have agreed as a society on several racial categories - although not everyone agrees on the categories, and they have changed over the years – (see Sidebar (pg. 35) for an example). In other parts of the world, racial categories are drastically different.

For example, in Brazil there are far more racial categories than in the United States. Although there is no significant biological difference between different races (see Sidebar "Scientific Proof" – pg. 28), most members of society have accepted a "constructed" reality where people with a certain skin tone are considered 'black' and another skin tone are considered 'white' (or yellow or brown or red, etc). We have further constructed an agreement about the values attached to each of those 'races.' Therefore, we treat people differently based on skin tone. While it can be useful to have a shared definition for concepts, such as "Please hand me the white paper," it can be very damaging to attach values to people, especially when they take away their individual identity. For example, "You are a bad Asian boy," strikes a very different chord than "You are a bad boy."

[social construction]: an idea or set of ideas that society has agreed upon together.

GOOD HAIR DAY

Not all dark skinned people have "bad hair." I remember the first time I let my hair out naturally and curly my freshman year. It was just another ordinary day for me, however this didn't seem to ring true for some of my classmates. I didn't expect people to make any comments because where I grew up, having curly hair wasn't something intriguing. I felt like since I grew up in such a diverse community, I was already exposed to many different people. I simply assumed that other students also experienced the same exposure; however, I was mistaken.

I received several compliments just walking from my dorm to the dining hall. I quickly noticed that most students were extremely fascinated by the volume and texture of my hair. This fascination had bothered me a little. It wasn't like I dyed my hair a random color; I just left it out curly. That was the first time I realized that most of the students probably had a different upbringing than me. I had to stop and realize that not every town is as diverse as mine and that our backgrounds have in fact molded the way we characterize and react to people.

I remember hearing later that day that there were a couple people that were debating whether my hair was all mine or not. I was furious because I knew my hair was all mine and more importantly I didn't wear my hair natural for it to be up for debate.

I didn't let my anger show until this boy called me out in front of a group of kids. He started out by saying, "I didn't know your hair can be like this." I responded by saying, "Like what?" I remember he said something along the lines of, "You know... not bad. I didn't know black people can have naturally curly hair."

I usually let ignorant comments slide, but I felt the need to address this one. I didn't want to be tokenized as the only black girl with "good hair." I remember telling him that even though human beings are all a part of the human race; every

> " I didn't want to be tokenized as the only black girl with "good hair." "

(26)

individual has a slight difference in their genetic make up, which determines their appearance. Just like every other ethnic group, black children take on different traits from their parents.

❝ *Racism has always been able to come up with a scientific veneer.* **❞**

— Andrew Hacker, 1992

Scientific "Proof"!

For several hundred years, scientists have been trying to prove that different races have significant genetic differences. Occasionally, a study will emerge that 'proves the point' the scientist is obsessed with. However, within a few years, each of these studies have been disproven when more closely examined. For example, Dr. Samuel Morton concluded in 1844 that Europeans were at the top of the intelligence chart due to larger skulls and therefore bigger brains as compared with non-Caucasians from around the world. When the exact same skulls were remeasured in 1980 by Stephen Gould, however, (read more in *The Mismeasure of Man*) it turned out that the skulls all had about the same volume. The difference? Perhaps Morton - the white scientist who used peppercorns to measure skull volume- packed them more tightly into the skulls of Caucasians, thus "proving" what he expected to find all along. The conclusion of reputable scientists today is this: while genetics might predict your hair texture or eye color or skin tone (though not always perfectly), it is not a predictor of intelligence, athletic ability or personality. There is no biological basis for the values attached to race. Why do you think it is important to scientists or the public for there to be a scientifically significant difference between the races?

Questions: Please reflect on the piece you just read and answer the following questions.

- ❏ Why might the boy in this narrative have thought black people don't have 'good hair'?
- ❏ Has anyone ever used your physical appearance to 'racialize' you?
- ❏ Have you ever used someone else's physical appearance for the same purpose?
- ❏ In our society, who has the power to determine what is 'good' or 'bad' for groups of other people?
- ❏ If the boy did not say his comment out loud, would it still be interpersonal racism?
- ❏ Does your appearance match society's expectations?
- ❏ Has this had a positive or negative impact on you? How so?

ACTIVITY The author of this story responded to a derogatory comment calmly and with a biological fact. Think of a time you've experienced or witnessed interpersonal racism. Now brainstorm two ways that you might have responded to the situation.

❝ *Do I need to appear "black," in the manner in which blacks are negatively portrayed in the media, to be considered "black?" ... I am an educated, well-spoken black woman. My race is one of my many attributes: neither limiting, nor defining. I represent the culmination of my experiences, and the many cultures that have influenced me. I represent the colors of my ancestors. But most of all, I represent myself, and of that, I am most proud.* **❞**

–Renee Delphin, 1997

THE REAL DEAL

I can be whoever I want to be

That's fine with me.

If it's not who you want me to be,

Then what is it that you see.

My color is not important

Look inside of me.

Can you find something?

Is there anything that makes you happy with me?

Should I change where I come from?

Or change my accent?

Maybe I should change my clothes

Since you think I look like an accident.

Questions: Please reflect on the piece you just read and answer the following questions.

❏ The author mentions several 'markers' we use to assign race and/or ethnicity to people (clothes, accent, etc.) What are some other markers?

❏ Have you ever incorrectly assumed someone's chosen racial identity? Has your own been misperceived?

❏ Is it possible to ignore someone's skin color? Is it desirable to do so?

❏ How do racial identity and ethnic identity relate to and complicate each other? Have you seen these issues connect in your personal experience?

ACTIVITY On a piece of paper, brainstorm 10 ways you can determine someone's racial identity.

1. _____

2. _____

3. _____

4. _____

5. _____

6. _____

7. _____

8. _____

9. _____

10. _____

Now go back through your list. How many of these are based on biology?

❝In my version of the Promised Land, I would not eliminate race, but I would eliminate the pecking order to which it is so closely tied. I have no idea what meaning, if any, race would acquire once it was detached from issues of privilege and power… but for now at least, I would be happy to just let it evolve.❞

— Harlan L. Dalton, 1995

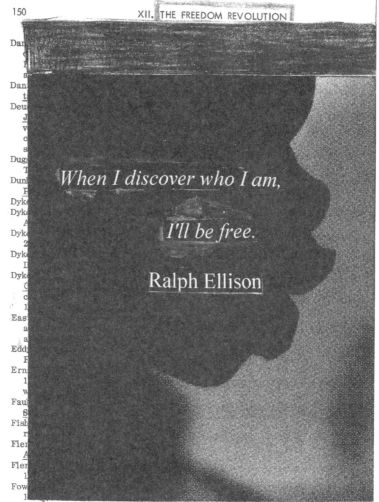

Galtung, Johann, "A Model for Studying Images of Participants in a Conflict: Southvi Journal of Social Issues 15:38–43 (October 1959). Study of a typical Southern com which actively resisted 1954 Supreme Court decision, designed to determine wha of images each of three groups (segregationists, integrationists, Negroes) has of other groups.

Gilbert, Arthur, "Violence and Intimidation in the South," Social Order 10:450–456 (December 1960). Relationship between prejudice against Negroes and anti-Semit

Glenn, Norval D., "The Role of White Resistance and Facilitation in the Negro Strug Equality," Phylon 26:105–116 (Spring 1965).

Good, Paul, "Klan Town, U.S.A.," Nation 200:110–112 (February 1, 1965). On Bogalu Louisiana.

Good, Paul, "Birmingham Two Years Later," Reporter 33:21–27 (December 2, 1965

Goodwyn, Larry, "Anarchy in St. Augustine," Harper's Magazine 230:74–81 (Januar

Hayden, Tom, "The Power of Dixiecrats," New University Thought 3:6–16 (Decembe January 1964).

Hays, Brooks, A Southern Moderate Speaks. Chapel Hill: University of North Caroli

ARE YOU MEXICAN?

Being Latina in a private school often causes me to feel insecure and angry due to the amount of ignorance that is constantly shown. When I first arrived at my school, I tried talking and interacting with several other new students. Being a predominantly Caucasian school, I was the only Latina there. One of the boys from my group asked me: "Are you Mexican?" I looked at my t-shirt which had the word "Peru" imprinted on it. I was hurt and bothered by his statement because of the ignorance he showed. This occasion was not the first time I have been called Mexican or spic in a preparatory school. Even my closest friends who know of my Peruvian heritage continue to call me Mexican. I have nothing against Mexican people, however, it pains me to see so much ignorance in such a highly educated school.

> **This occasion was not the first time I have been called Mexican or spic in a preparatory school.**

Questions: Please reflect on the piece you just read and answer the following questions.

❑ Why is it important for your friends to be aware of your ethnic, cultural, or racial heritage?

❑ In this story, people are trying to assign an identity to the author. Why do you think they feel the need to do this?

❑ Have you ever had someone try to assign an identity to you? How is this experience different than identities you choose for yourself?

❑ Is everyone allowed to choose their own racial identity?

(SURPRISING FACT) *Did you know that 'Mexican' was added as a racial category for the 1930 Census? After the addition, the Mexican government complained, and it did not appear in the 1940 Census.*

THE IMPORTANCE OF IDENTITY

That day was no different from the others. As my friends and I made our way down the hallway after lunch, still laughing about the conversations we had, we heard one girl walk into the bathroom and ask her friend, "Did you see all those black girls making all that noise?" I couldn't believe what I just heard. I remember thinking; did she really just say that? How was the noise we were making any different from the noise other groups of friends were making while leaving the lunch room? Lastly, I thought to myself, I am not black. Naturally, I was upset when I heard the girl ask that question, but I didn't know how to react. Should I have said something to her? Should I have asked her what she meant by asking that question? Should I have made her aware of the fact that I am not black?

Though I have attended [my school] since the sixth grade, I had never really thought too much about forming my own identity in a school where I was very different from the rest of my classmates. This 9th grade encounter, for lack of a better word, was the first time I really stopped to think about my identity and what it meant to be Latina in a predominantly white school. I never realized, before reflecting on that day in the hallway, that I was being categorized and placed into this box; I was one of the black girls. If there is one thing that bothers me the most about my school and other independent schools, it is the fact that Latino students are incredibly under-represented. There are often fewer of us than there are black students, so we are all just considered black by those who do not take the time to differentiate between us.

It is a fact that the Latina girls and the black girls in my class are close friends, because despite the fact that we are different, we can relate to the same issues when it comes to the ignorance we face in these schools. We also recognize that we too are different from each other, and understand that we experience ignorance towards our cultures differently.

I remember going to a surprise birthday party once with my best friend from school. We were two of the four people of color there, I was the only Latina, and she was the only black girl. Being at this party was no different from being in school, so I was not surprised to be one of the few minorities there. I was comfortable being there until word got back to me that someone made a comment about my friend and me. He said, "What are those two girls doing here, shouldn't they be walking around serving drinks or something?" I was really hurt to hear about that and wanted to say something so badly, but it was not my party and I did not want to make a scene and confront him in front of everybody. I let it slide and tried to continue having a good time.

Unfortunately, that was not the only ignorant comment I would hear that night. When taking a picture with my friend and the only other two people of color at the party, one boy remarked, "I want to be in the black people picture!" There it was again; I was just another one of the black kids. This time, I wasn't going to let it slide and I said, "I am not black, I'm Dominican." The boy stood in front of me and tried to shrug it off and say that, "It's all the same." This infuriated me. Why wouldn't anyone take the time to realize that Latinos and black people are not the same, have different cultures, and even within their own races have different ethnic traditions and cultural values. I was not alone in my anger; my best friend stood up for me and told him that it was not okay for him to say that we were "all the same" or to completely ignore me when trying to explain how I was Latina, not black.

> **Why wouldn't anyone take the time to realize that Latinos and black people are not the same, have different cultures, and even within their own races have different ethnic traditions and cultural values.**

Since the party, I have strongly identified with being Latina. I realized that if I didn't wear my identity on my sleeve then I would just be labeled as one of the black girls. Though I am a student of color, I think that it is so important for Latino and Latina students to identify with their culture and who they are in order for others to recognize the difference between Latino students and black students. Though most of us can relate to each other, we are different. If Latino students continue to let themselves be categorized as black students, we will remain under-represented. We need to let our voices be heard; we have to share our cultures with our classmates; and most importantly, we have to be proud of being Latino.

Unassimilable

In the 1990 U.S. Census, Latinos (the government calls them Hispanics) were re-classified from a race to an ethnicity. Census racial categories over the last 150 years have included: Chinese, black, Japanese, Mulatto, Korean, Mexican, Quadroon, Indian, Hindu, and Octaroon, among others. While some of these sound funny, government race classifications are no laughing matter. In 1922, Takao Ozawa, a successful Japanese businessman raising his family in America for many years applied to become a naturalized citizen. The U.S. Supreme Court turned him down and declared all Japanese people "unassimilable", claiming that scientific evidence indicated that Japanese people were not white (whiteness was a requirement for citizenship based on the 1906 Naturalization Act.) The following year Bhagat Thind, a man born in northern India, applied for citizenship. Thind referenced Ozawa's case - noting accurately that the same "scientific evidence" stated that Northern Indians like himself were Caucasians. But in this case, the exact same Supreme Court Justices (nine white men) dismissed the "scientific evidence" and denied Thind's citizenship, claiming that the "common man" knew Thind was not white. In the wake of these court decisions, many Japanese, Indian, and other Asian landholders were retroactively stripped of their citizenship and property holdings. Takao Ozawa took his own life a few short years later, having lost his land and his belief in his adopted country.

Questions: Please reflect on the piece you just read and answer the following questions.

- ❑ Why does a person need to wear their "identity on her or his sleeve" in order to avoid being put in a specific racial category?
- ❑ How can groups of specific ethnicities come together to let their "voices be heard?"
- ❑ Why do you think the white boy in the story refuses to accept the narrator's chosen ethnic identity?
- ❑ Why is it important for Latina/o people (or any other ethnic group) to be fully represented?
- ❑ What is your ethnic identity?
- ❑ Do you feel supported by your ethnic identity or is it something that gets in your way?
- ❑ What are the characteristics (positive or negative) associated with it?

INSTITUTIONAL RACISM

Our world is made up of institutions. Schools, libraries, businesses, government offices, prisons, fire departments - the list goes on. These institutions combine into larger groups we call systems - the education system, the healthcare system, the criminal justice system, the legal system, the governmental system, etc. When individuals act out their internalized beliefs one-on-one, there is often little impact beyond that pair of individuals. However, when individuals are given the power to act out their beliefs on a larger scale, the impact is far greater.

Since people shape institutions, develop their policies, and staff them, it is not surprising that race becomes a factor. Laws were put in place based on the prejudices and beliefs of the time, but even if they are no longer enforced, their legacy has a huge impact on our culture and practices. Just as The Declaration of Independence does not include women, so were many of our institutions founded to serve specific populations. One of the problems is that institutions change very slowly, but the populations they serve can shift quickly.

The Speak Up! Stories Project focuses on an institution that is essential to the development of our personal lives and our society as a whole. Schools are the place where we spend almost half of our waking time, the place where we rely on others to help us learn our values. The personal stories in this book serve as a resource for educating ourselves in a world where racism is very much alive.

(SURPRISING FACT) *Did You Know that it took nearly 10 years for Native Americans to successfully lobby the City of Boston to repeal a law that banned Native Americans from being within city limits (without an escort of 'two musketeers'). The law was repealed in 2004.*

When Susie Guillory Phipps applied for a passport in 1977, she started a 10 year legal battle that highlighted how the United States law has been used to racialize Americans. After receiving a copy of her Louisiana birth certificate, Phipps discovered that she was classified as "C" for Colored. Upon hearing the news, Phipps took to her bed for three days. An extensive geneological review revealed that Phipps was 1/16 African-American by heritage, despite having lived as a white woman for her entire life - attending white schools, marrying white men (twice) and bearing 'white' children. Perhaps in anticipation of the impact this ruling might have on her and her family, Phipps sued the Department of Health and Human Services for 'white' status. While Phipps lost all the way through the Louisiana Supreme Court, she might have chosen a simpler route to whiteness - moving across the state lines to Mississippi, where the law classified a person as black only if 1/8 or more of their decedents were African-American.

If you were the judge, what would you rule in the Susie Phipps case? Do you believe the law should regulate race?

THE LIBERAL INSTITUTION

Because I thought [my school] was such a liberal and welcoming community, I really did not think any racism or ignorance could ever be present. I assumed that such a prestigious and upstanding private school of high academics would be aware of other cultures around. I also assumed that every school member, especially the faculty, would acknowledge the small percentage of students who are not white and do not come from a steady, wealthy household. I am Vietnamese-American. I am an immigrant. I was born in Vietnam and came to the United States when I was two years old. I learned to speak both Vietnamese and English simultaneously. I do not live in a big house and my parents do not drive fancy cars. My parents work everyday of their lives so I could focus on school. I can confidently say that I have worked very hard in my studies. I strive to do the best I can for my sake as well as my parents'. As a result, I was accepted to my school, an all girls private school.

The majority of the students and teachers at my school are white. Only a small percentage represents the minority students and an even smaller percentage represents minority teachers. During freshman year, I was taking an English class called Expository Writing. It was a huge class. I sat in the back of the class with another minority student because there was not enough space to fit two more desks in the circle apparently. At the time, I did not realize the effect of how a small thing such as seating arrangements had upon me.

As a freshman, I was more worried about the workload and everything that came along with officially being in high school. I remember this one time I had a one-on-one meeting with my English teacher. We had just finished writing another paper for this week and he was handing it back to me with corrections

> " I sat in the back of the class with another minority student because there was not enough space to fit two more desks in the circle apparently. At the time I did not realize the effect of how a small thing such as seating arrangements had upon me. "

and comments. We went over thesis statements and content and it was going fine. Halfway through our meeting, he said something that made me feel so angry and so offended.

Because of a few grammatical and mechanical errors, he told me that it is understandable because I am not from this country and I am "foreign" to the way things work in this country. He talked to me like I was some inferior, illegal alien from some poor, third world country that cannot measure up to some "white, American standard." I was so angry that I could not even say anything. I just stared blankly at his oblivious face and listened to his condescending words. A part of me was too scared to say anything because at that time, I was not confident in myself at all. I was intimidated by the "prestige" of my school and all its academic standards. Because my school is so "liberal," I could not believe that teachers, of all people, could be so completely ignorant and rude.

I guess even in a community like my school or anywhere else, there are always going to be certain people that would put you down. Of course I am not saying that my school is this superficial, unsafe environment for people of color, I just believe that there are certain people who still blatantly judge others by what they see. Maybe I was too quick to judge my school on its liberalness after all.

Questions: Please reflect on the piece you just read and answer the following questions.

❏ In your own school, have you observed different expectations being placed on students of different cultural, racial or ethnic groups?

❏ Do you personally have any different expectations for different cultural, racial, or ethnic groups?

❏ How might teachers help any student deal with issues of racial identity without singling them out and making them feel uncomfortable?

❏ How is institutional power present in these interactions?

Pair up with two or three people and make a power map of your institution. Where is the power collected? What are some of the outside systems and institutions that have an influence on your school? Who creates the policies of your institution?

A Step Further: If you wanted to change something at your school, how would you go about it?

IT'S MORE THAN STUDENTS

I always knew private schools tried to make an outreach into lower income areas to get diversity in their school, but until one Wednesday I thought they truly cared for those kids. I now understand that kids who are minorities are not treated as individuals, but instead what those schools consider a means of showing off. I was staying late at school one day, and noticed the teachers having a meeting in the conference room right next door. I noticed on the screen they had a list of different schools around the area and the level of diversity in their school. It occurred to me that if they solely cared about helping out kids who are minorities, their concern would not be what they looked like next to other schools, but that is what it was. They wanted to be able to say, 'Look what we have, and they don't.' To that school, those kids were simply a way of attracting parents who wanted to pretend like they had a nice mixture of ethnicities at their kids school.

I also had a friend, who was black, and another who was white. We had a reputation for not fully cooperating with the teachers for challenging their ideas, which was not what the school wanted. We would constantly get in trouble for absurd reasons that we could not even understand, and it was pretty clear the faculty actually did not have too much of a reason either. Sometimes we would hang out with the kids in the grade below us and we would mess around, so the teachers would give us suspensions for what they called bullying. As if that was not bad enough, the teachers blamed my black friend for getting us in trouble saying he was a bad influence on us. They solely blamed him for problems that were barely even real, treating us as if we were innocent and had no mind of our own – it was absolutely disgusting. I also happened to know that he had better grades than we did, so unless this was discrimination I saw no reason behind their actions, and that action was completely and utterly based on racism. They push to get diversity, then discriminate against the kids they bring in who they use as a means of bragging.

Questions: Please reflect on the piece you just read and answer the following questions.

❑ What are the benefits of programs in schools that specifically aim to increase the enrollment of students of color? How have these programs' intended goals been reached in your school (if applicable)?

❑ The author mentions being targeted and unfairly punished at their school. Have you seen examples of students in your school being unfairly targeted or punished?

ACTIVITY Think of a specific time when you saw a teacher or administrator treat you or someone else unfairly, or a time when a teacher or administrator made a comment that you found "absolutely disgusting" or offensive. What did you do? If you are unhappy with your response, what might you have done? See our Strategies Section for some helpful hints!

A Step Further: What are some ways that you can address institutional injustice in your school?

Carmack, William R., and Theodore Freedman, <u>Factors Affecting School Desegregation</u>. New York: Anti-Defamation League, 1962.

Carter, Barbara, "Integrating the Negro Teacher Out of a Job," <u>Reporter</u> 33:31-33 (August 12, 1965).

Clark, Dennis, "Color and Catholic Classrooms," <u>Integrated Education</u> 1:9-15 (June 1963).

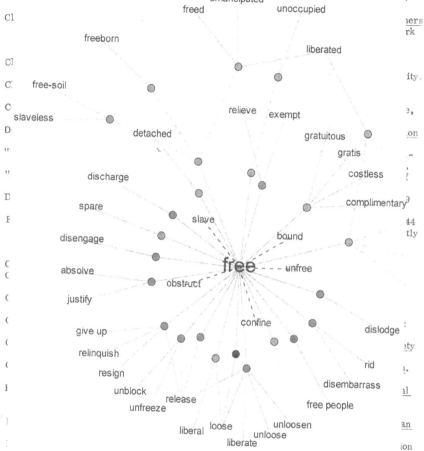

"Integration in Public Education Programs," <u>Hearings before the Subcommittee on Integration in Federally Assisted Education of the Committee on Education and Labor</u>, March 1, 1962-June 15, 1962. U.S. House of Representatives, 87th Congress, 2nd Session, 1962.

Johnson, Guy B., "Progress in the Desegregation of Higher Education," <u>Journal of Educational Sociology</u> 32:254-259 (February 1959).

Kenealy, William J., "Desegregation," <u>Social Order</u> 12:249-256 (June 1962). In a debate with William F. Buckley, Jr., editor of <u>National Review</u>, Father Kenealy advocates use of federal power to combat segregation.

IDEOLOGICAL RACISM

[ethnicity]: of, or relating to, large groups of people classed according to common racial, national, tribal, religious, linguistic, or cultural origin or background

Ideology and Culture are nearly indistinguishable concepts, as both terms capture a set of shared beliefs, ideas and values. Yet an ideology is more than just a shared set of beliefs - it is also the process by which those beliefs are shaped. Imagine you are watching a large school of fish, individual tiny silver-white arrows, moving in apparent unison. With no perceptible or sharp movements, the school changes direction, each one responding to the tiniest shift around it. Each fish represents a system or an institution or a powerful individual, pushing and pulling, shifting and being shifted by cultures and belief systems. Those at the front may shift long before the back has taken a turn. Occasionally a fish veers off course or strikes out in a new direction, but mostly they hang together.

Now imagine that you are one of those fish, swimming at the front edge of that school. Ahead of you, you think you can see safety, or nourishment, or a healthier world. Yet your neighbor keeps nudging you to go to the right. What would it take to resist this push and swim off in your own direction? What if you were wrong?

Ideologies have the power to 'define reality' and the power to 'set the norms, standards and values that govern others' behaviors.' Imagine you are the fish in the very center of that school. You can no longer see safety or food, your reality is a mass of silvery bodies. Trying to turn in another direction is nearly impossible, your behavior is governed largely by others. If you've always been part of the school, then you may not even be able to envision another reality.

American ideology from the founding of this country held the belief that European Americans (whites) were superior in every way to all non-whites. They could not have subjugated, dislocated, and killed millions of the Native Americans already living on this continent without that belief. All of the institutions founded in that time were created within this ideology (including schools and universities). All of the decisions and policies at those institutions were made with this belief in mind which still impact students today. Even the Civil War was fought not because President Lincoln believed everyone was equal, but because he believed a divided nation could not stand against others. Institutions and policies can change - but slowly. Even as the front of our school of fish shifts slowly toward equality, the back of the school is still not sure which way to go. Ideology casts a long shadow.

If we can not recognize the cultural norms and ideologies that operate in our world, we run the risk of allowing them to determine our behaviors for us. We have ideologies about race, gender, money, sexuality, national identity and many more. Ideologies are expressed by individuals, institutions, systems, our families, our friends, and the media. As you read these stories, think about your own ideology and how ideological racism might have an impact on your life. Think also about the institutions and systems that are transmitting, maintaining, and enforcing ideology.

VOTING ON YOUR VALUES

The 2008 presidential election was truly the first time that I've paid attention to race. The main reason was obvious: it was the first time a man of color and a woman had run for president. At school, I felt like a lot of the juniors and seniors who were eligible to vote voted for [Barack] Obama, and a few of them voted for [Senator John] McCain. My feelings toward things vary. For a while, I was a supporter of Obama, but when someone asked why, I only had one answer: because he's black! I stopped following the election afterward, because I realized that it hadn't become about politics and the good of our country. When Obama was declared president, a few underclassmen verbally expressed their discontent. So ask yourself this... for the people that voted for Obama, was it only because he was black? And for the people that did not vote for Obama, was it only because he was wasn't white?

❝ *I couldn't believe I was going to spend the rest of my life fighting with people who hate me when they don't even know me… Why should I have to keep getting my face smashed? Why did I have to prove what no white man had to prove?* **❞**

—Sammy Davis, Jr., 1989

Questions: Please reflect on the piece you just read and answer the following questions.

- ❑ Do you think race, gender or ethnicity should be taken into consideration when voting for a politician?
- ❑ Should lawmakers take race or gender into account when crafting laws?
- ❑ Should school administrators factor race or gender into curriculum?
- ❑ How do race, ethnicity, gender (religion, ability, age, etc.) affect public policy and governmental systems?

ACTIVITY Below are nine squares. In each square, write a part of your identity that is important to you.

Do you have nine identities written down? Now imagine that the government just told you that you must eliminate the identity that is least important to you. Look through your list. Which one would you give up? Why?

A Step Further: Continue the activity by crossing off the identity that is least important to you until you have only three identities remaining. Circle these three identities and then continue reading. Now cross out two of them, leaving the identity which is most important. Which is it? Why?

Affirmative Action

The laws pertaining to Affirmative Action are an example of politicians taking gender and race into account when crafting public policy. In 1961, President John F. Kennedy issued an Executive Order stating that government contractors must "take affirmative action to ensure that applicants are employed, and employees are treated during employment, without regard to their race, creed, color, or national origin." President Lyndon B. Johnson added 'sex' to the list in 1967. The intent of this executive order was to affirm the government's commitment to equal opportunity for all qualified persons, and to take positive action to strengthen efforts to realize true equal opportunity for all.

These orders were passed because there was a clear pattern of certain groups being discriminated against. Since these laws were passed, there has been an increase in access for several classes of individuals (though there is still clear discrimination - see Sidebar 1 for more information on subtle discrimination.) Who has been the number one beneficiary of Affirmative Action policies?

ANSWER: White women are the most frequent beneficiaries of Affirmative Action.

SEPARATION

Racism is everywhere, you just can't see it. Some can't feel it and some barely even know it exists, but those people may be unconsciously using racial slurs. However they come out as jokes, the jokes are instrumental in the separation of "races." At my school, when you walk into a free seating lunch, you will instantly see the separation. There is a Mexican table, there is a Korean table and there is a black table. After that, however, you see things spread and it's just friends sitting with friends. The separation could be considered racism, or you can call it comfort. Not many people are willing to step outside of their comfort zone.

Questions: Please reflect on the piece you just read and answer the following questions.

❏ Why does sitting with people of your own race keep you in your 'comfort zone'?

❏ Is forced integration an effective tool for combating racism?

❏ What are some ways you might respond if you hear someone making a racist joke?

❏ Are people segregated along lines of race during lunch at your school? What are the benefits and detriments of self-segregation? What action might the author take to de-segregate a lunch table?

❏ What kind of ideology encourages people to make racist jokes?

ACTIVITY Brainstorm two ways you can get outside your comfort zone around issues of race.

A Step Further: Read Beverly Daniel Tatum's book *Why Are All the Black Kids Sitting Together in the Cafeteria.* Why are all the black kids sitting together in the cafeteria? This book highlights the racial identity development of students of color and white students, and helps explain the impact of ideological and cultural racism on our daily lives.

WHO'S A TERRORIST?

When I was a sophomore in high school, I took a class called Overview of American History. It was a fairly typical course, meant to acquaint 15 year olds with broad themes in our nation's past. We covered everything from the Thirteen Colonies to the cultural and political upheavals of the 1960's, but one period stuck in my mind more than any other: Reconstruction. While discussing the post-slavery south, the Ku Klux Klan came up, and my teacher, in addressing their role called them terrorists. This caught me a bit off guard, but the term fit. Like the people blowing up hotels in Baghdad, trains in London or skyscrapers in New York, the Klan was a group that targeted and terrorized innocent civilians.

After that class, I examined 10 history textbooks and they all referred to the Klan as a hate group, but only one used the term terrorist. Conversely, in discussing the 1993 bombing of the World Trade Center, all of the books I examined used the term terrorist to characterize Khalid Sheikh Mohammed and his co-conspirators. When I thought about it, I could come up with only a few white Christians who our society and especially our mass media classifies as terrorists. Timothy McVeigh (of the Oklahoma City Bombing) and Randy Weaver (of the Ruby Ridge Shooting) come to mind, but mostly white terrorists in our country seem to remain faceless, nameless, and free. While every single Arab, Muslim or Sikh in our country goes through daily harassment, thousands of white power terrorists live their lives largely free of governmental or societal scrutiny.

The reality is that both a small number of whites, and/or Christians and a small number of Arabs and/or Muslims are terrorists. I believe that most Americans would not commit the sort of heinous acts associated with both the Ku Klux Klan and Al Qaeda. We should not make the mistake of thinking that the actions of one of these groups is any more forgivable than the actions of the other. Both are terrorist organizations and it is only when we see both as equally evil that we will be able to begin building a world that does not tolerate the sort of hate that ethnic and religious terrorism engenders. By using teaching literature that tries to minimize the damage done by the Klan and other domestic terrorists, schools create a hierarchy of evil. Hate is hate whether it comes in hooded white robes or turbans; it's time we as a society called a spade a spade.

Questions: Please reflect on the piece you just read and answer the following questions.

❑ Who has the power to define what a 'terrorist' is?

❑ What ideology frames Muslims as 'terrorists' and Christians as 'hate-groups'?

❑ While it is obvious who is hurt by this ideological framing, who benefits from these distinctions? Why do they persist in our institutions/media?

Smith, T. Lynn, "The Changing Number and Distribution of the Aged Negro Population in the United States," Phylon 18:339-354 (Fall 1957).

Taeuber, Conrad, and Irene B. Taeuber, The Changing Population of the United States. New York: Wiley, 1958. A volume in the Census Monograph Series, prepared for the Social Science Research Council in cooperation with the Department of Commerce. With emphasis on the period 1890-1950, white-nonwhite differentials are presented on such matters as rates of growth, migrations and urbanization of nonwhites, marital status, families, education, fertility, and mortality.

Taeuber, Irene B., "Migration, Mobility and the Assimilation of the Negro," American Negro at Mid-Century, Population Bulletin, Population Reference Bureau, Inc., November 1958. The fundamental change in the Negro population has been not so much movement from South to North as the concentration in industrial areas in all sectors of the country.

Taeuber, Karl E., and Alma F. Taeuber, "Changing Character of Negro Migration," American Journal of Sociology 70:429-441 (January 1965).

Valien, Preston, "General Demographic Characteristics of the Negro Popula____ in the United States," Journal of Negro Education 32:329-33_ (Fall 1963).

Wattenberg, __, This U. S. A.: A_ unexpected __il_ ___trait of 194,067,2__ ___ricans Drawn ____ _ Census. Ga___ Ci__ __. ___ ___ d or_ _65 Census _____ stati__ __ in c_ aborati__ ____ ___ar__ S____, D____r, _. S. B___ _f the ____ ___ly ch___

We have to talk about liberating minds as well as liberating society.
Angela Davis

Th_ ___ ___ ___ ___ ___ssistance of Alex Ha__ ___ King, Jr. Chicago: ___nnett, Lerone, Jr. ___ders various
Johns_ ___

INTERNALIZED RACISM

We have now read a number of stories which involve interpersonal interactions - where one person says something hurtful to another. Whether these occur within institutions or in the greater world, we must ask the question: What causes these interactions? Why would someone intentionally hurt another person? One answer is that they are living out their internalized beliefs, their personally held perspectives. For example, James Blake (the bus driver in the Rosa Parks case) may have believed that white people were superior, and that they deserved to sit at the front of the bus. That is an internalized belief, picked up from the ideology of the time. However, had he worked only in a white area of town, and had only white passengers, he might never have had the interpersonal interaction that helped spark the Montgomery Bus Boycott. He still would have had the internalized racial superiority, it just would not have been acted out.

The other way internalization is expressed is via internalized racial inferiority. What impact does repeated exposure to negative media images and negative messaging have on young people of color? In the late 1940's, psychologists Kenneth Clark and Mamie Clark conducted an experiment in which young black children were given the choice of playing with a white doll or black doll. These young children preferred playing with the white dolls, and used positive language to describe them while using negative language to describe the black dolls. Their findings were instrumental in arguing the Brown vs. the Board of Education case which overturned legal school segregation. Chief Justice Earl Warren wrote in the Brown v. Board opinion, "To separate them from others of similar age and qualifications solely because of their race generates a feeling of inferiority as to their status in the community that may affect their hearts and minds in a way unlikely to ever be undone."

Sadly, that study was repeated just a few years ago with similar results. Another recent example was described in the Sidebar "What's in a Name?" (black and white names and resumes) and serves to reinforce the idea that employers are acting out their internalized beliefs with a serious systemic impact. Whether we look at internalized racism from the perspective of superiority or inferiority, the impact on each of us is deeply detrimental to our psyche, our health, our employment, our education and every other aspect of our lives.

HAIR

I barely remember what it was like to have natural hair. I have vague memories of my mother combing my hair and complaining about how thick it was and how it was so difficult to manage.

What I do remember is crying because the old metal pressing comb always slipped out of Mrs. Henry's hands and burned my scalp. I remember being so excited to get my first relaxer in 5th grade, and crying yet again because the burns on my scalp from the lye was something I hadn't been warned about beforehand. I remember feeling rejected because no one wanted to play with my hair in middle school because it was "greasy" and even after the hours I sat in my salon to straighten my hair, it was still too stiff to be as good as theirs. I remember feeling embarrassed about having to avoid rain, swimming, and sweating because my hair would revert back to a semi-natural state.

I know the rhetoric about black hair. It's easier to manage if it's straight; it's just too thick and nappy in its natural state. I also remember how hard it was in a predominantly white high school to be black, constantly feeling pressure to live up to an impossible white aesthetic. I hated my hair, hated my blackness, and hated that I could never feel good enough. I constantly hid the complicated and absolutely painful processes I went through to approximate white hair, pretended that I was just like them, and never saw how problematic my thinking was.

Last year, I cut my hair. I grew out the oppressive, painful, damaging, disgusting chemicals and never looked back. I have come to love and embrace my hair, and believe that I've taken an important first step to undo all of the wrong thinking that I gained over the years. I'm completely natural, and have never been happier.

Lye is a corrosive compound, which damages organic tissue. It is used in oven cleaner and drain opener. It is recommended that lye not be stored in glass containers, as it will slowly eat through them.

Questions: Please reflect on the piece you just read and answer the following questions.

❑ Why are young women of color encouraged to have straight hair? Who is encouraging this?

❑ Besides not being able to swim or sweat, and the cost of hair treatments, what other negative impact does this pressure to conform to white standards have?

❑ Have you ever been uncomfortable with your identity? Why is this? What has caused you to want to change yourself?

❑ How can you become more comfortable with and proud of your identity?

SHAME

A person feels shameful when they have said something uncalled for, unnecessary, or possibly hurtful to another. They feel shame when they messed up on a musical piece, on stage, or out on the field. Shame creeps up through the spine when the guilt can no longer sit still and contain itself. Shame overflows out of your ears, slides out your mouth, and punches your stomach, to remind you that somehow you screwed up, made a mistake, did something wrong. So why, sitting there in the stuffy building that smelled of deodorant and sweat, did I feel this dreaded emotion? What did I deserve to be shameful of? The way my hair curled up, eyes stayed deep brown, or for the color of my skin? All things that I have no control of, and cannot escape. Things that are visible at first glance, allowing others to judge me before they even know my name. So sitting there, as others stared right through me, I was forced to bow my head in embarrassment and shame, for just being me.

> **"** What did I deserve to be shameful of? The way my hair curled up, eyes stayed deep brown, or for the color of my skin? All things that I have no control of, and cannot escape. **"**

When we were released from that bland building with cold wooden benches, some members of my community had already forgotten the words that were spoken to us less than five minutes prior. Other people's laughter clogged my throat, as I realized that much of what was said was already stuffed and crammed to the way back of the minds of my classmates. What scared me even more than this ignorance and denial was the fact that day after day I was forced to gather in the same building and sit among the person who had wished death upon me and my family on a dirty bathroom stall. I was a new student at the time and had hoped I would learn to find security and trust in my new school. But as I walked to my next class, feeling alone and vulnerable, I knew that my safety had permanently been sacrificed.

My school tried calling some attention to the racist remark, but referred to it as an "incident," which had everyone walking on eggshells around it, and eventually had me using that term along with them. This made me grit my teeth, and burn up inside, but I accepted it, and to cope just hid deeper into myself where I knew I was safe. Though I did appreciate some response, the conversations we had just ended up alienating the black kids and leaving some of the others feeling totally excused and unrelated. People kept insisting it was only one person, which felt to me like a way to disregard the extremity of the situation. A part of me still feels that the reason my school addressed it was because there was no clear culprit behind it, and they knew they would never find them, so they didn't really try. This would have allowed them to know that eventually it would be easy for them to sweep it under the rug.

I can honestly say that I have never been in the bathroom, that those bitter, salty words were written in. I think it is out of fear that even after being scrubbed away, I would see right through the stall and relive my shame as I read, "I want all niggers to die."

Questions: Please reflect on the piece you just read and answer the following questions.

❑ What impact did this hate-crime have on the author? How did they internalize the message written on the bathroom wall?

❑ If you knew the author of this story, how might you support them?

❑ How can you work with others across racial boundaries to ensure that people are not alone in their battle against racism?

❑ What impact might this incident have on a school community?

ACTIVITY Beside an assembly, what might the administration in this story have done to address this issue?

❝ *I think that rage is an understandable and appropriate response to an absurd situation, namely, black people finding themselves in a situation of white supremacist power.* **❞**

– Cornel West, 1997

"Here was an ugly little girl asking for beauty... A little black girl who wanted to rise up out of the pit of her blackness and see the world with blue eyes."
Toni Morrison, <u>The Bluest Eye</u>

Katz, Irwin, and L. Benjamin, "Effects of White Authoritarianism in Biracial Work Groups," <u>Journal of Abnormal and Social Psychology</u> 61:448–456 (September 1960).
Kelly, James G., Jean E. Ferson, and Wayne H. Holtzman, "The Measurement of Attitudes Toward the Negro in the South," <u>Journal of Social Psychology</u> 48:305–317 (November 1958).

BETTER THAN?

I'm thinking back...

My class has one African-American student out of 250. He plays football; I don't even know his name, and I've never talked to him. We never sit at the same lunch table. He was never in any of my honors or AP classes.

My school has one Indian-American student out of 1000. He was quiet. We were both in the play together, and he always seemed to look up to me. I remember one day I did a card trick - he would pull out a card, look at it, and I would immediately guess what it was. How come he never figured out I was seeing the reflection off his thick glasses? Everyone else knew what was happening.

...

All my teachers are white. All my friends are white. All the kids on the other teams are white. Everyone who does anything good in my life is white. I guess that's just the way it is, maybe white people are better than. Maybe I'm better than...

...

What a horrible thought! Where did that come from? How did this thought creep into my head? Am I a bad person? Am I a racist?!?

...

Wow. Am I a racist? Really? Truly? I guess the simple answer is no.

...

The complicated answer is probably "yes". I do have racist thoughts, reinforced by my life experiences, my time in this all-white school, my town, my sports teams, my family, the media, my friends... I guess I have been 'racist-ized' by my country. Can I live my life without acting out some of those beliefs and thoughts? No. I guess I do sometimes treat people differently based only on the color of their skin, and maybe even think in my deepest heart of hearts that I have some sort of superiority.

I hate this system, I hate the impact it has on me. I hate how it forces me to act sometimes. It takes away my humanity. I can't treat my peers like human beings when my every action has all this power behind it. I hate this system.

Questions: Please reflect on the piece you just read and answer the following questions.

❏ The author mentions some examples of personal times they started to develop a racially superior attitude. What are some institutional or systemic causes of this attitude?

❏ What is the impact of internalized racial superiority on the author?

❏ What might this author do to change how they live out their internalized beliefs?

❏ What sort of ideology supports the development of this perspective?

ACTIVITY What are some of the internalized perspectives you are proud of? What are some of the internalized perspectives you are not proud of?

A Step Further: What might you do to change how you act out your internalized beliefs?

DIVERSITY IS BULLSHIT

My school emphasizes diversity a lot. We talk about it a lot. But I sometimes wonder if it's bullshit. The general sentiment here is that we are not racist, we are not sexist, we are not homophobic, and we are so much more accepting and open-minded and tolerant than anyone else.

> **66** I hate the word tolerant because it implies there is something to tolerate. **99**

I hate the word tolerant because it implies there is something to tolerate. When people say that as if it's a compliment, I know they don't mean it like that but I still want to throw up. And I wonder if secretly people are only putting up with me.

I'm from South Korea and so are many other kids here. I remember freshman year people were surprised at a cute group of dark haired boys and girls. They even wrote an article about "The Koreans" in the school newspaper.

Some people used to say, "Why are so many Korean kids here?" because they didn't realize they were being horrible. "Well, I don't know, I would say," and secretly scream, Well, it's not my fault, it's not our fault. They accepted me and so I came; I came to a school where teachers don't hit you or one entrance exam into college decides your future.

I bet they still say it, though, just not in front of me.

I think here if you're American and you fit into the borders of what's considered the norm – and those aren't just about race – you have, automatically, a certain degree of respect. You are an individual. You are Allison or Daniel or Eliza or Jack.

But I think for me, I have to earn it. I gotta take hard classes and get good grades and make art and write for the newspaper and play sports and be in plays and be on student council and do community service and do very well on standardized tests.

Then, I won't be just "the Korean kid." I'll be something else, at least while I'm doing something. I do so much for this school and so do my dear Korean friends. We do different things. When people say, "You guys are all so..." even if it's in good context I want to yell at them. And then, I hate myself for saying things like "We are...".

Sometimes someone tells me not to reinforce the Asian stereotype. Maybe I shouldn't talk about home so much. Do people sigh when I start "Well in Korea, we..."? I can't be feminine because again I reinforce that geisha stereotype. I need to speak up in class and speak lovely English without an accent, and loudly, because Asians shouldn't be quiet and obedient!

I know no matter how many years I live here I will never be like everyone else. Something will always be a little off and I'm very proud of that. I just wish everyone else knew that.

Questions: Please reflect on the piece you just read and answer the following questions.

❑ What is the impact of internalized racial inferiority on the author?

❑ Sometimes someone tells the author "not to reinforce the Asian stereotype". Why might someone suggest this? Is this helpful advice?

A CLOSER LOOK:
SPECIAL TREATMENT OR SAFE SPACE

We hope that by now you are thinking about the many complexities of race and racism. If it was as simple as laws being passed or people no longer using hateful language, we'd probably have moved well beyond race in our world today. Unfortunately, race is still as complicated as it was 350 years ago, when Virginia lawmakers were passing the laws to keep white, blacks, and Native Americans separated or the Constitution writers using the word "all others" in 1787 to refer to slaves and Native Americans.

Today we have very different perspectives on some of the major issues facing our country – such as global warming, immigration and education. No one strategy will satisfy everyone; no one approach will work for everyone. In the two stories that follow, we have two students of color who have very different responses to the age-old idea of a 'safe space' – a space where people can gather around a shared identity to do whatever they need to – to vent, to grow, to support one another, and to think about their next steps. While these are not the only two authors who talk about segregation and safe spaces, they capture two sides of a multi-faceted argument very well.

[discrimination]: prejudiced or prejudicial outlook, action, or treatment

SEPARATE, BUT EQUAL?

I never thought of myself as a "Student of Color" until I came to my new school. I have never been a victim of racist or demeaning comments, and I have never noticed any differences between my predominantly white classmates and me. The second I walked into the new high school, and even the summer before, I received all sorts of invitations to events specifically for "Students of Color." It is the fact that I was automatically categorized as different that made me realize something; in trying to celebrate the diversity of students, my school's plan to do so backfired and instead further separated the "Students of Color."

My school definitely emphasizes the idea of the diversity of the student body. There are clubs and programs dedicated to promoting diversity of the students. However, there is one flaw that I see in these organizations that really upsets me. I believe that in creating such clubs and organizations, the school categorizes the "Students of Color" into their own group, and therefore defeats the purpose of the clubs in the first place.

You might be asking yourself, "How is this possible if these clubs are dedicated to promoting diversity?" First of all, they automatically send "Multicultural Newsletters" and emails regarding diversity events to the "Students of Color." If the whole point is the unity of all students, then why are only students of color being forced into clubs and events such as the "Multicultural Student Barbeque," an event created to ease the transition of new students of color into the school. Who says that students of color are in need of more help with the transition to a new learning environment? Why not invite the entire new student community to the barbeque? These are the types of questions that I ask myself whenever I get an email regarding such events.

Another example of this special treatment of students of color that outraged me is the "Diversity Checklist." One day while I was looking through my emails, I found one with the subject "Diversity Checklist."

I opened it, and at the top of the page it read, "This email will be forwarded to all of your teachers and your advisor." As I scrolled down, I saw a list of questions that would be sent to all my of my teachers; amongst them were questions such as, "Is this student regularly participating in his/her class activities?" and "Is he/she completing his/her homework efficiently and on time?" I could not believe what I was seeing. It is sad to think that organizations that advocate the equality of all students send out surveys to make sure that only the "Students of Color" are doing well in their classes.

Do not get me wrong. I am all for the appreciation of different cultures and traditions. Our ethnic backgrounds are a huge part of who we are as people, and I believe that it is essential to celebrate different cultures and traditions, but the fact that certain students are treated differently (even if it is meant to be beneficial) because of the color of their skin truly frustrates me. All students want is to be treated equally, and by creating special events for "Students of Color," we are only moving away from reaching the goal that we are working so hard for.

OUR SAFE SPACE

Though [my school] tries its hardest to be an open community and celebrate diversity, there has never really been a change in social dynamic. The jocks still hang out with the jocks, the brainiacs with the brainiacs and the artists with the artists. Most social groups are comprised of only white people. In the alcoves, there is always one called, the "black alcove" because that is where most of the African Americans hang out. But where do we Asians go? Most Asians feel the need to fit in, even though they are clearly a minority group. They normally do not hang out with each other. They break off and go into mostly white groups and try not to show any cultural differences besides the color of their skin.

Every month, there are [women of color club] meetings, where all the female students of color come together and just hang out. I find myself never going to these meetings, mostly because I am busy, but also because when I think of this club, I think that it is mostly a group for African American females, talking about their issues regarding their color. Even though I know that it is a group for all women of color, I find myself passing on these meetings. I know that my case is not always the case of others, but many others have the same thought process when deciding whether or not to go.

This is the reason why we created [an Asian-specific club]. It is a group that meets once a month, comprised of only Asians, where we talk about our own cultural issues and school dynamics, and pressures of being Asian. We also talk about the stereotypes and how accurately we fit them/ don't fit them. Though this is not a way to make my school more of an accepting community, it helps us connect more to each other and embrace a culture that isn't embraced during school.

SECTION WRAP

These two stories highlight that our institutions have a long way to go - and that there are many different perspectives to address racial disparities. One author finds the effort of administrators to be offensive and insufficient, while the other has sought a new and supportive space to explore issues of culture and race. One rejects segregation as divisive while the other embraces segregation as a healthy structure. The following questions explore this concept more deeply. The activity is designed to help us reflect on ways our institutions might not be supporting all students equally.

❏ What common ground do these authors have?

❏ What strategies can you think of that might meet both of their needs?

❑ Do you think a separate space for white students would be beneficial to help them address questions about their own racial identity?

ACTIVITY Think about your school. Who is in authority? What is on the walls? What language(s) are used? What music and food is available? Who has credibility? Who is treated with full respect? Whose experience is valued? Whose voices are heard? If the answer to these questions is consistently one group over another, what might you do to make your school more welcoming for all?

INTERSECTIONS AND IDENTITY

" *There is no such thing as a single-issue struggle because we do not live single-issue lives .* "

– Audre Lordé

" *One day our descendants will think it incredible that we paid so much attention to things like the amount of melanin in our skin or the shape of our eyes or our gender instead of the unique identities of each of us as complex human beings.* "

– Franklin Thomas

Many of the stories you have read in this book include more than just a single focus - the author may recount an interpersonal interaction as a springboard to understanding. As we have seen elsewhere in this book, our identities have many different facets. Race has an impact in our lives, but so does our gender, our wealth and class, our perceived or actual sexual orientation, our physical abilities, our access to education, our age, our education. In the society we live in today, race is one of the most visible of our identities, but it is certainly not the only one that provides us (or others) with meaning. Our work against racism is of paramount importance, but we must remember that our issues, like our lives, are connected. Though these stories only touch the tip of the iceberg on a few of the many ways our identities intersect, we hope you will start to think about the interchanging of your many identities and how they can shape your experiences.

UNTITLED

Young, black, and male, a combo perfect for oppression. My small private school in Boston agrees. Unlike the rest of the world being male at my school marks you as a possible trouble maker. Add black into the mix and its game over. Over my time there, being one of four black males, I've been targeted in every possible way. Whenever any thing goes down at school, me and my friends are always the ones who are looked at. We are public enemy number one. A school that prides itself on being a progressive, liberal and accepting place? It sure doesn't seem like it from where I stand. How is it that only being tangentially involved in a problem can all of the sudden make you the main aggressor? The bad guy?

A big group, guys and girls, out with their school in Maine play with fire making s'mores. Sounds like fun, just harmless fun. Then the shit hits the fan. Teachers screaming and girls are fleeing. Then the headmaster, the big boss, the detached hand of justice gets involved. And yet who does he address? Three black boys and their white friends. All boys. No girls. How is it that they, the females, can get by unscathed while I'm sitting in some office being all but told that I'm a terrible person because I was in the vicinity of some wrong doing? In the end it's the same ol' shit I deal with day in and day out. Nothing new. Nothing exciting. I am the villain I am in the wrong, I get it. I do not belong. From where I stand all I see is hostility, nothing even that overt. All I see is a bunch of passive aggressive assholes trying to say to me you do not belong. You do not belong within the confines of our "open" yet oh so closed community. I get it. I'm a marked man, me and my brothers we are marked men. Our school has tried its very hardest to get rid of us but we're still here sadly or maybe luckily only for just one more year. We are the last of a dying breed, our school has seen to that.

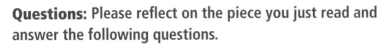

Questions: Please reflect on the piece you just read and answer the following questions.

❏ The author admits to being in the wrong place at the wrong time. The result is a trip to the headmaster's office. How does this experience compare to the story 'Whiteness' in which the author lies to the police and is let go without a questioning look?

❏ The author notes that he and his two friends are the last three black boys at their school. What is the impact of this on other students of color? On white students?

THE OTHER F WORD

Words. Their use, powerful. Gook, chink, nigger, wetback - all words used to bring people down. For me, the most affecting word is faggot; the other F word. It makes my blood boil. Gives me an adrenaline pump to absolutely pummel the person who said it. Being LGBT (Lesbian, Gay, Bisexual, Transgendered) is a lifestyle I am proud of. It is who I am. In my school, the word faggot can be somewhat of a term of endearment. For me this is not the case. Having "_____ is a faggot" written on the bathroom wall was the most heartbreaking thing I have ever seen in my life. Seeing my name associated with that word disgusted me. I wanted to cry and scream, but I kept my composure. I would not let this word bring me down. I will not let this word bring me down. I am stronger because of this word.

Questions: Please reflect on the piece you just read and answer the following questions.

❑ Where does the power in these words come from?

❑ Why do people use words which disparage someone else's identity?

❑ How can people deal with hurtful words and comments if they are not given the chance to confront their author?

ACTIVITY Did you complete the activity after the story "Voting on your Values"? In it, you wrote nine meaningful identities down, and crossed them off one by one. You should have three that are circled. Look at the last two that are crossed out. How do they intersect with the identity not crossed out? Where is there overlap? What happens when one identity is threatened?

A Step Further: Think about the way that this author describes the impact of words that are hurtful to her/his identity. Can you think of a time when you felt this way about an identity that you hold dear?

PART OF YOUR WORLD

To my surprise, my freshman year in high school was really tough for me. I think I just might not be a part of THE world here. I can't remember how many times, I met one of my friends here, we say hi to each other, and we walk away.

I can't remember how many times I sit with a bunch of people, while they're talking, I just sit there, wondering if I could say anything. I can't remember how many times that I felt left out in a conversation, I seemed too tiny that can be easily ignored, so just standing in the crowd, feeling really lonely. I can't remember how many times I sit in the cafeteria, seeing people that I know walk past me, without saying a word. My English is not that good, so that often I can barely understand jokes that people tell. I laugh when the crowd laughs. I felt that I was just a timeserver, I hate to do that, but I have no choice. I can't ask people what does it means when it's SUCH A SIMPLE WORD but I just can not understand it. I think that's part of the reason why I have so few friends. I know that things like these take time to change, but although I'm working on it, I still have no friends.

It might not be a big deal for any of you, but it's a big deal for me, because I never ever experience such thing called lonely. I used to have a lot of friends, we used to do everything together and I can barely imagine how life would be without them. I used to smile not cry a lot. I've always hope someone could come, and take me away, he might be the god, I don't care.

I am a bisexual. And when I first find out that, I was scared. I was afraid that people talked about me staring at me in a weird way. And more importantly, I'm afraid that I can't get over it. But there's always someone beside you when you need help. He helps me get over it, talks to me when no one talks to me. And it's no longer a problem now, I just treat it as part of my soul.

I choose not to tell my parents about these whole thing. They love me so much, I know they'll feel worried and I don't want them to feel bad because of me. They have to afford the heavy private school fee, and are worried about getting fired.

I am trying to be more confident, more brave, more happy, and that's another whole long journey. So I want use a quote to end this story.

" *There's always something, something good, something worth for you to use the rest of your life to get, so please smile, and keep walking.* **"**

Questions: Please reflect on the piece you just read and answer the following questions.

❏ What role do parents play in someone's security about their own ethnic, racial, gender, and sexual orientation?

❏ How does language and accent play a role in how certain people are treated?

❏ What can schools do to create an environment where people feel safer to come out? How can individuals create a safe environment for their friends to come out?

There are few things in the world as dangerous as sleepwalkers.
Ralph Ellison

TAUGHT TO KILL

It was a month into school. I was a new student, still with a glossy high school image in my head. I wanted to believe everything about my new school was perfect, and it was where I belonged. I wanted to love all the people, love the classes, and the intellectual discussions we had.

I signed up for Model UN, and was eagerly checking the conference on our email system. People were openly debating ideas on many different topics, and one thread came up about religion, and religious camps for children. The conversation went on as people presented different ideas, and I began to get nervous as the emails discussed Islam and Christianity.

As I read one of the emails, I was shocked into passivity. "The difference is, one person wrote, "Christians are taught to love, and Muslims are taught to kill."As a student, this appalled me. As a Muslim, it stunned and stung me. How could someone be so ignorant and insensitive? How could he think this was true, is this what he truly believed? Could he say that to my face? If he knew I was Muslim, would he believe I had been taught to kill?

Other students responded quickly, pointing to his discrimination and using the crusades as a counter example, showing Christians too have had pieces of violent history that they may not look back proudly on. But I couldn't say anything. It was such a sensitive issue for me that I didn't even feel I could rebut his ignorant remark. Just knowing there was one person that was confident enough to make that assertion kept me from telling him his email hurt me, and I didn't feel I could even express my religion and have him truly understand. So I let the other students take control, putting him in his place because they knew it was wrong. It meant a lot to see other people reacting in this way, even if they didn't truly know how it felt to read those words, but it sometimes makes me angry how helpless and passive I felt, just from the words of someone my age at my school. All I could think of was that phrase, "Christians are taught to love, and Muslims are taught to kill." I was too scared to expose myself as a Muslim, I felt too vulnerable to say anything to my defense and instead I tried to shut it out of my head.

Eventually, the club moderators announced they were going to delete the entire thread, as it had been getting out of control and too attacking and personal. So just like that, all the emails were gone. There was no more discussion, no conversation, no repercussions.

There are fundamentalists in every religion, people that twist the message and ideas of a religion. But they do not represent the entire religion, nor the majority of followers. I don't understand why a group of terrorists can be associated with an entire group of people, and how our culture absorbs this issue. It is unfair, and hurts me.

I am not extremely religious. I do not pray five times a day, don't fast for Ramadan in school, but I do believe in God. My religion is something I don't talk about a lot. I'm not ashamed. However, I feel ashamed that now every time I tell someone I'm Muslim, I watch their reaction carefully. Sometimes people seem surprised. I guess I don't talk about it a lot. When I tell people I don't eat pork, I never tell them it's a religious reason unless they ask specifically why I don't. And that's when I watch their response. I think I am always sub-consciously afraid that someone is going to want to distance themselves from me after knowing I'm Muslim. I'm afraid the media has influenced everyone to the point where they look at Muslims differently. When the media shows a bombing scene in Iraq and pans over a mosque with people bowed down in prayer, this is the kind of negative associations that get into people's heads, these are the messages that stick subconsciously so when someone sees a brown man with a turban and mustache boarding a plane with a briefcase, their heart quickens ever so slightly. Unfortunately I know there is racism and stereotypes which have become engrained in people, even in this liberal blue state. So ignorant people exist, like this stupid boy that sent the email.

There are smart, intelligent, and empathetic people in our school. But the fact that there was even one student who could say what he did and get away with it without knowing how much it hurt me and made me feel unsafe? That is what has to change.

Questions: Please reflect on the piece you just read and answer the following questions.

❏ It is often difficult to tell someone's religion unless they self-identify. If you have a religious practice, in what ways does it intersect with your racial or ethnic identity?

❏ What happens if someone is in the marginalized group of one aspect of their identity and in the powerful group in another?

❏ What role does the media play in stimulating or continuing racism and should the media be held accountable?

ACTIVITY Pretend that you are one of the moderators for this email list. Brainstorm four ways that you could have acted differently to engage the students in a healthy discussion.

A Step Further: Think about the issues that came up in this story around open discussion. Brainstorm four ways that you can start an open, honest, and healthy discussion with your peers about tough topics, or how to facilitate this type of discussion when issues arise freely. Feel free to use this book as a starting place!

VISIONS

This section is dedicated to your vision of what you would like your school to look like. Before we go on to strategies, it is important that you have a sense of your ultimate goal.

- What do you want to get from your school environment?
- What type of atmosphere do you think would be more open?
- If you could create the ideal school, what would it look like?
- What classes would be offered?
- Who would be in power?
- What would the social dynamic look like?
- Where would you fit into this community?

Brainstorm about your "ideal" school; feel free to use the space provided. This will help you decide what strategies you want to use to ultimately achieve this goal.

Ways you can share your vision:

- ❏   Write out answers to the questions above.
- ❏   Make a mind-map or brainstorm.
- ❏   Create a collage.
- ❏   Write a story about your ideal school environment and post it to our Blog (www.speakupstories.org).
- ❏   Draw a picture.
- ❏   Do something creative we haven't considered...

SHARE YOUR VISION!

SHARE YOUR VISION!

Our grandfathers had to run, run, run. My generation's out of breath. We ain't running no more.
Stokely Carmichael

STRATEGIES! EDUCATION! RESOURCES!

This book was not only created to reveal the hidden truths about racism in our institutions, but also to act as a guide for those inspired to take action. Everyone can begin working on strategies. Any effort, no matter how big or small, will make a difference. You just need to take the first step in addressing the injustices you see in your own life, community, and school. Below you will find a story from one of our editors. You will also find some strategies that you can start working on. Don't forget though, working for justice can be hard and lonely. We encourage you to work with others. Working with a team increases your power and helps you stay focused while thinking creatively. Feel free to be inspired with your own strategies!

We have also listed multi-media resources in this section as a way to give you back-up as you take on some of the strategies listed here, to name and dismantle racism at your school, in your community, and everywhere it's found. You'll find websites and contact information for organizations that support antiracist work in Boston and around the country, as well as suggestions of books, documentaries, online tools, and other media that address race and racism.

We are more prepared to challenge racism when we have the tools we need, such as help from other people and lots of information. Use these resources to strengthen your work and your group's work, whether you are engaging people in conversations, organizing a campaign, educating others, or whatever responses to racism you dream of and carry out!

{A note to readers} Our list of strategies was brainstormed and tested by a multi-racial team. As a result, some of these strategies might seem better for one racial group or another. For example, 'stepping out of your comfort zone' may be a great suggestion for white people, but a place people of color find themselves more often than they'd like. Be sure to pay attention to everyone's voice when thinking through strategies and action steps, and check in often with everyone to make sure they are working for all!

Just as these stories have looked deeper at different aspects of racism, so do our strategies take into account different ways of addressing racism. Some are more effective at addressing interpersonal racism, some at institutional racism, some at multiple forms. At the bottom of this page, you will find a key indicating which area we think a particular strategy will be most effective.

You will notice we have laid this section out with Strategies on one side of the page and Resources connected to those strategies on the other. This is a simple way for you to put these strategies to use – or get more information if you need it! You'll also find three more stories – because none of this happens without stories!

And now, a **Call to Action**!

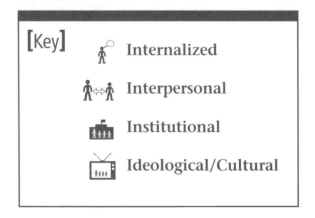

[Key]

- ☝ Internalized
- 👤⇔👤 Interpersonal
- 🏛 Institutional
- 📺 Ideological/Cultural

RESPONSIBILITY

I, as a white person, have a responsibility to work on racism. I cannot say what people of color need. I cannot solve the issues that I think are most prudent to people of color. I can act as an ally. I can hear and thoughtfully listen to the issues raised by people of color and act as a support. An ally by definition means to combine or unite a resource for mutual benefit. The word "mutual" is key. I am not only helping people of color, but people of color are helping me. By taking action against racism, as a white person, I am taking a stance against injustices.

I am working on this book because I cannot not work on it. I cannot hear my classmates' stories about their experiences and not act on the impulse to take action. I do not comprehend what a person of color goes through every day in our society, so I need these stories to help me understand. I cannot say that people of color need this book, but I can say that I, as a white person, need this book. I need this book to confront the truths of the institutions and society that I am living in today. I need this book to give me solace that people are taking action.

This book, to me, is more than a reminder of the racism that exists in our schools. It is also a reminder that the action of white people is an important aspect in the work against racism. Assuming the role of an ally has historically been proven essential to a cause. There is power in numbers.

I hope to all you reading, especially those white peers feeling somewhat overwhelmed and questioning their own reasoning to take action against racism, you understand the importance of your power. I am a white person working against racism. If you feel at all moved by any of these stories, join in the cause. Like I said before, if you become an ally, you will benefit, probably more than you will sacrifice.

HOPE

As an African American, I cannot deny racism because its consequences are what I am required to deal with on a regular basis. I have often noticed that many white people don't like to talk about race. This is because they don't have to. Racism is a load that I am disproportionally forced to carry. I need to remember that this is not my sole responsibility. We need to stop looking at racism as a problem of "us" versus "them," because with this view people of color are always "them" and consequently it is always "their" problem. Discrimination damages everything and everyone. Ironically enough, it is color blind in the sense that it hurts all who it touches, or who choose to touch it. Just as racism affects us all, we need to collectively work on fighting against it. As a person of color it is important to acknowledge that it's not my job to speak for my race, or to educate ignorance at my own expense. I do not have to defend myself or my experience. I'll never stop fighting but I will not beat my fists in midair and talk to a wall. I will do what I can and hope that the humanity of others, which transcends race, will help do the rest. It is my right to be heard and be safe.

It gets tiring to be told that racism does not exist despite my personal experience that says otherwise. Racism is deeper than forced segregation, deeper than the south, deeper than the N word. I am working on this book because a personal story cannot be denied. Every story in this book is real and valid and to deny this is to deny that the authors hold truth. It is to deny that they count. To those reading this, I hope you realize that you are not alone. In your pain, in your guilt, in your struggle. I hope you find comfort and solace in hearing stories of those brave enough to speak up, and this gives you the courage to do so as well. I hope you are motivated and inspired to take action, keeping in mind the idea that racism is a burden we all must carry. When spread out amongst many, each person carries a significantly lighter load.

- Educate yourself. Be knowledgeable about systemic injustice in your community and beyond. Refer to the suggested readings, questions, and activities that we've mentioned throughout the book. Talk with teachers, friends, family and community members. Hear stories, engage with history, and read!

- Educate others about all that you have learned and read (awareness is essential!). Try to meet everyone where they are. Engage them through their stories and your own. Lecturers rarely make friends!

- Attend anti-racism training workshops, through Sub/Urban Justice or other organizations, to about learn non-violent action, leadership, as well as organizational skills.

- Remember that Sub/Urban Justice and Boston Mobilization offer specialized workshops using the Speak Up! Anthology as a starting place. Contact us today to learn how you can bring Speak Up! to your school! Contact Chris at Chris@BostonMobilization.org or call 617-492-5599. Or visit us online at www.bostonmobilization.org

Race: The Power of an Illusion Website and TV Documentary Series by the Public Broadcasting Service (PBS) and California Newsreel

▶ **Check it out!** "*Race: The Power of an Illusion*" is a 3-part TV documentary series about race in society, science, and history and it has an accompanying interactive website, complete with links to articles.
  • Go to www.pbs.org/race

▶ **Watch!** The series is available for sale online and is a very effective introductory teaching tool about race as a social construct with destructive consequences. Find out if your school, local library, community organization, or church has a copy or would like to order it.

Focus on Affirmative Action by the African American Policy Forum

▶ **Listen!** This think tank, the African American Policy Forum, has posted on its website a series of audio programs that debunk myths about Affirmative Action.

1. Visit www.aapf.org/focus

2. Select an episode from the list on the lower right-hand side of the page.

3. This will take you to a specific episode. Then follow the instructions and click to listen. The file should automatically begin playing in mp3 format. (Note that not all episodes have audio available.)

4. The episode websites also include facts and figures, quotations, and additional suggested reading.

The November 3rd episode debunks the myth that "individual effort and hard work determines who becomes prosperous and wealthy in the United States."

▶ **Use it!** This November 3rd episode includes an interactive exercise called "Starting Line" which allows participants to act out how race and ancestry have impacted wealth accumulation in the United States.

1. Go to www.aapf.org/focus/episodes/nov3.php

2. Find the "Mythbusting Homework" section towards the bottom of the page

3. Click where it says "The exercise is located HERE"

Still want more?

Try this: *List of Additional Websites and Reading Materials* by Peggy Riehl

▶ Peggy Riehl is an Early Childhood Specialist who maintains a webpage that includes a myriad of links to publications and websites on diversity, anti-bias, anti-racism, and multicultural education, many of which are youth-centered.

1. Go to http://home.sprintmail.com/~peggyriehl/prmulti.htm

2. Click on the links that interest you and you can access many useful materials.

- Get involved with an organization (at school or outside of school) that is working on these issues you care deeply about.

- Start your own organization (at school or outside of school). If you want help planning an organization, please contact Sub/Urban Justice (www.suburbanjustice.org) for more information.

  Sub/Urban Justice has helped young people from across the greater Boston area start clubs or organizations to take action on issues that matter to them. In the spring of 2009, Sub/Urban Justice graduates in Boston started an organization called BPS Student Alliance for the Future of Education (BPS SAFE) to address budget cuts in their schools. They formed a coalition with other teen groups and met with the Superintendent, the School Committee, the Mayor, the Governor, and eventually their legislators. They asked for the legislature to pass new laws giving Boston more local revenue. Two laws were passed, granting Boston the right to tax its meals and hotels an additional percentage and keep the revenue. This teen coalition has demanded that a significant percentage of this new revenue be put toward their schools. Teens CAN take action to make a difference, and having an organization support you can be helpful.

- Make sure your school and community have the resources they need to challenge racism. If you live in Boston or nearby, consider visiting the Yvonne Pappenheim Library on Racism, hosted by Community Change (www.communitychangeinc.org).

- Support your peers and encourage them in anti-racism work. No one wants to do this work alone.

- Create support groups. No one can do this work alone. Make sure to see our list of school contacts and diversity resources at various AISNE schools!

▶ **Get in touch!** These are groups organized to address racism and its impacts locally, regionally, or nationally. They use different tools and strategies to do this work, and can be resources for people learning about how to dismantle racism. Look them up on the internet or give them a phone call to learn more!

Charles Hamilton Houston Institute – Cambridge, MA – The Charles Hamilton Houston Institute continues the work of one of the great civil rights lawyers of the 20th century.

125 Mount Auburn St, 3rd Floor, Cambridge, MA 02138
http://www.charleshamiltonhouston.org/Home.aspx

Crossroads Antiracism Organizing and Training – The mission of Crossroads Antiracism Organizing & Training is to dismantle systemic racism and build anti-racist multicultural diversity within institutions and communities.

P.O. Box 309 Matteson IL 60443-0309 Phone: 708.503.0804
info@crossroadsantiracism.org   http://crossroadsantiracism.org/

The People's Institute for Survival and Beyond – New Orleans, LA and Nationwide – PISAB is a national and international collective of anti-racist, multicultural community organizers and educators dedicated to building an effective movement for social transformation. Here is the contact information for the national office of PISAB:

Ron Chisom, Executive Director • Tiphanie Eugene, Administrative Director
601 N. Carrollton, New Orleans, LA 70119 Tel: (504) 301-9292   www.pisab.org

▶ **Other great groups!**

INCITE! Women of Color against Violence – P.O. Box 226 Redmond, WA 98073   Tel: (484) 932-3166
email: incite_national@yahoo.com   http://www.incite-national.org/

Visions, Inc: – 48 Juniper Street, Roxbury, MA 02119-1749   Tel: (617) 541-4100
email: office@visions-inc.org   http://www.visions-inc.org

Catalyst Project – 522 Valencia St #2, San Francisco, CA 94110
email: info@collectiveliberation.org   www.collectiveliberation.org

Even More: The Aspen Institute maintains an extensive list of organizations doing work to dismantle racism all over the United States. A quick trip to this website can get you connected to an incredible number of people doing amazing work.

1. Go to http://www.aspeninstitute.org/policy-work/community-change

2. Scroll down; on the bottom left , click on "Structural Racism Resources"

3. Click on "Tools for Dismantling Structural Racism"

4. The list of organizations and groups should appear at the top of the page, with their addresses and descriptions of what they do below.

STRATEGIES – DISCUSSION

Discussion is an important part of addressing racism. If we can't talk to each other, we can't begin to build the relationships we need to challenge racist institutions, systems, and ideologies.

- Share the stories, reflections, and questions in this book with friends, teachers, and community members to get conversations started. Encourage people to react to the stories by speaking from their own experiences. 🧍↔🧍

- Publish an article or story in your school or town newspaper to get a conversation going in your community. 🏫
  Want to write a letter to the editor but haven't done it before? Here are some pointers:

Dear Reader,

Heres how to write a successful letter to the editor:

First, think of a topic or a new idea that has not been brought forth. Use your own knowledge and experience to make a concise argument (newspapers usually want less than 250 words). Be sure to write your name and what school you attend or community you live in – this might be critical information that sets your comment apart from others. Also, make sure you indicate that your letter is exclusive to that newspaper. Newspapers prefer to print original content. Be as direct and straightforward as possible. Share your perspective, but understand that this might create controversy. Controversy is good! By stirring up your community, you will enable people to talk about issues they were unable or uncomfortable to discuss before. The more people talk about it, the more successful your letter/article is.

Sincerely,
The Speak Up! Staff

Here is one more story. It is also a resource!

LUNCH TIME

As a student in a course focused on dynamics of race, class, gender and privilege, I wondered how to bring discussions of oppression and privilege to the rest of my school community. Hoping to move from discussion to action, I worked with three other students to map our cafeteria. We asked students to place an image of themselves where they normally sat and explain why they sat there. We created this project to push people to think about the space they are in, their identities in relationship to others, the boundaries that are created both consciously and unconsciously, and how community is formed. We wanted our peers to understand the social and political implications of space. Curious and uncomfortable, students asked, "Why are you doing this?"

The map revealed patterns of social dynamics that are rarely discussed. We asked our peers to consider whether race, class, and gender affect friendships. The responses varied from "I sit with people who speak the same language as me" to "I sit with my friends." The point of this project was less the actual words on the map but more the process of thinking together. I did not expect people to write their deeest thoughts about social dynamics on the map. Instead, this project prompted people to take a moment to reflect on their choices and actions and the reasoning behind these. I believe that thinking about race and class starts by acknowledging both our own racial and class backgrounds and our prejudices. It is then that we can have dialogue. We asked people to become conscious, to open their eyes, and to examine themselves.

I find the dynamics of my cafeteria especially interesting as a student who attended public school in the diverse city of Cambridge. Automatically, dynamics change when an environment shifts to a

Picture of Washington D.C. Mall – Read the artist statement about this artwork (p. 11) and then start a discussion about the effectiveness of the Civil Rights Movement in ending racism.

predominately white one. Based on the map it was clear that many international students sat together, many Latino and Black students sat together, and white students sat together. Of course, this is a generalization and a complicated one to make. A person could say "students of color sit together" but an equally accurate interpretation might be that white students choose to sit with other white students. Of course, among both white people and students of color, social dynamics occur based on class. These dynamics are less obvious and visible. Nonetheless we all look for people with common experiences or people who can empathize and work to understand our own identity struggles, and yet often white people unconsciously join with others based on the experience of familiarity and privilege.

This dynamic of joining together around commonalities is neither good nor bad; but it can become exclusionary when we are no longer open to or curious about those unfamiliar to us. In the project of raising consciousness and questions, I wondered what was next. How do people decide to both understand differences and find commonalities? What allows students with disparate histories and experiences to work to understand "the other"?

Nine strategies for facilitating a good discussion:

1. Listen to understand! Don't plan your next response - if you are hearing what someone is saying, dialogue happens naturally. It is critical to keep an open mind because your opinions might just be changed.

2. Sharing personal stories (like those in this book) helps others to understand where you are coming from.

3. Asking "Why?" is a great way to go deeper. "Why did you feel that? Why is that important to you?" Questions are the opposite of assumptions!

4. Start close to home. It's a lot easier to talk to your friends about these challenging issues because you have a relationship with them. But if you don't eventually expand your perspective, you'll get stuck in a rut!

5. Talk about what brought you together. Why do you each care about these issues? What do you want to gain from this discussion and conversation?

6. Brainstorm. Combining all your knowledge and see what as a group you know. This will help you see what you need to spend more time on.

7. Use an activity. Look at the many activities from our resource section. After the activity is over you can debrief and talk about what just happened.

8. Discuss goals. What do you want to accomplish through this discussion? What main ideas do you want addressed?

9. Have fun!

Here are a few more resources with tips for leading good discussions on racism.

Race Matters and MORE Race Matters Toolkits by the Annie E. Casey Foundation

▶ **Use it!** The Race Matters and MORE Race Matters toolkits are available on the Annie E. Casey Foundation's website. These tool kits include discussion questions, fact sheets, guides, and data. They can be helpful if you're educating others about race, planning a strategy or next steps for a campaign or other work, and to deepen your analysis and understanding of structural racism.

1. Go to www.aecf.org

2. On the main page of the website, click on "Knowledge Center."

3. Search for "Race Matters Toolkits" using the Keywords search field.

4. Browse the list of documents, click on any of them you wish to read and use. You can also download a multimedia presentation and a "users' guide."

5. Give feedback and ask questions! Contact them at racematters@aecf.org

One America Dialogue group discussion tool by President Bill Clinton's Initiative on Race

▶ **Use it!** This is a document produced by President Clinton's 1998 Presidential Initiative on Race. It is a step-by-step guide for setting up and leading a community dialogue on race relations, with suggestions on ways to bring community members out to participate in a dialogue, discussion starters for difficult topics, quotes on racism, advice for how to establish a safe space for sharing, and more.

Go to:
www.racematters.org/oneamericadialogueguide.htm

More about how to make safe space for discussion:

Brainstorm a list of ground rules. Make sure everyone is in agreement. Perhaps one of the rules is that words cannot be repeated outside of this safe space (confidentiality). Another may be for everyone to respect other opinions and feelings. Play ice-breaker games to bond as a group.
For a list of icebreakers we use at Boston Mobilization, contact us at www.bostonmobilization.org

It is important for people to feel comfortable enough to share their feelings.

Get Personal!

Here are some important steps you can take to further the fight against racism.

- Acknowledge your own internalized ideas about race and make real steps toward change. Internalized white superiority and internalized racism are very different for different people, and can be painful to confront. Here are some general definitions to reflect on:

- "Internalized white superiority" has existed for many generations in the U.S., teaching white people to believe, accept, and/or live out the myth of white superiority and to fit into and live out superior societal roles.

- "Internalized racism" is the unquestioning acceptance of the myth of the racial inferiority of People of Color.

- Confront your privilege.

- Stand up for your beliefs. Do not be a bystander!

- Always keep a critical eye on systemic inequality-- not just racial inequality, but inequalities around gender, sexuality, ability, class, religion, and much more.

- You CAN make a difference! There are actions you can take with your friends, in your school at large, and in the broader community to address racism and its destructive impacts. We will list examples of things to do at those three levels. As you undertake this difficult work, please remember a few things:

It may feel uncomfortable to face racism, but remember, comfort only keeps the status quo. Discomfort is a sign of change and learning.

There are examples of youth organizing for power and positive change going on all over the US and even the world! Youth have been leaders throughout the history of such movements for racial justice as the struggle to end Apartheid in South Africa and the Civil Rights Movement in the U.S. It can be exciting and empowering to learn these histories of youth power- do a little research if you want to learn more!

- Want to know who else is doing youth organizing around the U.S. right now? Take a look at this online directory:

▶ Search! Enter an issue area or region of the U.S. to find youth organizations: **http://www.future5000.com/about/**

- Ready to take on big issues? The Student Environmental Action Coalition has several online guides and handbooks for direct action and applied power organizing.

▶ **Use it!** Download these guides for free! **http://www.seac.org/resources/online**

- Planning a direct action campaign? Curious about who has power over a situation and how they can be influenced? You can create a "power map" for your campaign to help with campaign strategy. The best way to learn to make a power map is from a person or group who has experience using this tool. You can also start by looking at this example of how to do power mapping online: **http://www.thechangeagency.org/_dbase_upl/tCA_power_mapping.pdf**

- Do you have a campaign planned and now you need to find more supporters? Try this online game to get familiar with knocking on doors in your community, which is a great way to do outreach and organizing: **http://organizinggame.org/**

- Work on specific issues that are manageable. Saying "I am going to end racism" is overwhelming. Instead, create small realistic goals that will work towards ending racism.

1. **Taking action with your friends:**

   - One way to address racism with your friends is by speaking up when you hear racist comments/jokes.

   - In the story titled Separation, the author talks about using jokes in a racial context. The authors of this anthology believe that no matter what the intention or rationalization might be, the most important part is recognizing the impact that people have on others. We advise that the readers take care to understand that everyone has a right to their own opinions, and should not have to feel verbally assaulted by others, no matter how the joke-teller might view the situation.
   We also understand that it is often very difficult to stand up when you're in a situation in which you feel verbally assaulted, so we've included some strategies that you can use when you feel the need to confront someone if something they say is hurtful, offensive, or just plain bothersome.

Try this approach to racist jokes:

1. Interrupt the racist joke. Do not let it continue or deal with it later.
2. Confront the person or group of people.
3. Make it personal. Explain why you feel offended.
4. Do not speak in a patronizing voice. Everyone is in a learning experience. Speak in a helpful and concerned tone.
5. Ask for a change. Regardless if the person was only joking, seek accountability.

How to plan a public demonstration:

1. Pick a topic about which you are passionate and feel strongly. Make sure you know WHY you're hosting an event. Is it to put pressure on a decision-maker? Is it to get more folks involved? Is it to get media attention?

2. Think about your location and time. Public places usually are the best because they can hold more people. Make sure you obey the law because some places need permits.

3. Advertise. Use flyers, emails, and word of mouth to get people active in this demonstration. Invite the local media.

4. Plan your speakers ahead of time. These speakers can have inspirational stories or important information. Make sure they can captivate the crowd!

5. Use posters and chants.

6. Set up an information table about the issue. Include flyers and lists of organizations working with you. Have information and a website where people can learn more.

7. Make sure you have a large group of people. Enlist support from your organization, friends, and people you think who are most affected by this issue.

2. **Taking action at your school**

   - Pay attention to school policies - what are the rules? Are they applied unfairly or unequally? Who is responsible for setting these policies? ⛪ If you discover a policy at your school that needs to change in order to continue your fight to dismantle racism, see the next page for steps you can follow to make that change.

3. **Taking action in your community**

   - Find out how racism affects people's lives near where you live. Search online, look for flyers at libraries, community centers, or on community bulletin boards, and talk to community members to find out what's going on! Remember, the effects of institutional racism often show up in many different parts of our lives, such as housing, health, jobs, education, and the prison system. ⛪

   - What are people already doing about these issues in your community? Get connected with this activism and see if you can help out.

   - Use our political system to create change. You can work with the government even if you cannot vote. Participate in campaigns and advocate. Meet with your representatives and press them to enact laws. ⛪ 📺

   - Organize public demonstrations or participate in other more dramatic events already organized. ⛪

How to change a policy in your school.

1. Learn about your issue. Make sure you are knowledgeable about your cause.

2. Form a committee. Get a group of students (and faculty) who will support you. Learn about Base-building and One to One's- methods for reaching out and building strong connections with people. There is power in numbers!

3. Research what is happening in your school. Who is in power? Who do you need to talk to for change? Who will be your allies and who your targets?

4. Raise awareness in your community. Get public opinion on your side.

5. Make your own policy recommendations - what's wrong with the policy as it is? What do you want to see different?

6. Make the ask. Propose a formal plan to those in power.

7. If they say yes, celebrate your victory! If they say no, you need to organize a larger group to apply the pressure. Also, do not feel discouraged. Many movements in history would not have been successful without sustained commitment.

8. Publicize the new change. The school will have to uphold their commitment.

9. Want to know how to plan a public demonstration? See the previous page!

Join Speak Up!

- Write your own story and share in our blog or with your community. It can be cathartic as well as a valuable learning experience.

- Visit the Speak Up! website and respond to the blog.

$$\left\{ \text{www.speakupstories.org} \right\}$$

- Ask for Speak Up! to come to your school and conduct a workshop.

- Join Sub/Urban Justice or Boston Mobilization. We offer an intensive interactive summer program: www.suburbanjustice.org. We also run programs in schools and communities throughout the school year. Give us a call to find out if we're in your area! (617) 492-5599.

For additional curriculum resources developed by teachers, please visit our website www.speakupstories.org. To schedule a student-led workshop or training using Speak Up!, please contact Chris@BostonMobilization.org.

13 ⁰But if he wi...
then he shall add a fifth *part* there...
unto thy estimation.

14 ¶ And when a man shall sancti...
his house *to be* holy unto the LORD,
then the priest shall estimate it, whe-

which ... LORD's. ...
be ox, or sheep; it is the LORD's.

27 And if *it be* of an unclean beast,

& 22. 30.
Numb. 18.
17

Of course, we don't have all the answers, and many of these strategies won't work exactly right in your school or community. So get creative and come up with your own ways to address racism. We've left you some space on the opposite page to brainstorm your own ideas. In the meantime, here are some other strategies people have used to address racism.

- The use of prayer, faith, and spirituality is a way that some people act against racism on a deeply personal level.

- Work on issues found in our Intersections and Identity section. Class, gender identity, religion, and ability are deeply intertwined with racism.

- Address racism in all aspects of your life, not just your school. Work with your family, town or city, or congregation.

- Become a Speak Up! Peer Educator!
  Email us for details – chris@bostonmobilization.org

SPEAK UP! CONCLUSION

Racism is tenacious. At different moments in history, people have proclaimed that racism was over or about to be finished off. But racism wasn't ended with laws banning the importation of enslaved Africans into the United States in 1808, or with the abolition of slavery in 1866, or with the Reconstruction Era in the late 1800's, or with the desegregation of schools in the 1950's, or with the Civil Rights Movement of the 1960's, or with Affirmative Action Policies of the 70's and 80's, or with the election of a black president in 2008. No problem that has lasted more than three centuries will be transformed in a week or month or year. But there is hope, just as there are actions we can take. There is also joy in taking action. For us, this project has been difficult and challenging. The stories and truths we must all face can be upsetting. Yet, knowing that we are making a difference and hopefully empowering you to take action is joyous. When this book is published and read by all of you, we will be happy. The work that you can do will be just as challenging and joyous as our work. We look forward to working with you to make this world a better place.

❝ *We can go on talking about racism and who treated whom badly, but what are you going to do about it? Are you going to wallow in that or are you going to create your own agenda?* **❞**

— Judith Jamison,
Alvin Ailey Dance Theater
Artistic Director, Performer

❝ *We cannot choose the color of our skin, but we can choose the nature of our beliefs.* **❞**

– Clyde Ford, 1994

CITATIONS

Bertrand, Marianne and Mullainathan, Sendhil. Are Emily and Greg More Employable than Lakisha and Jamal? A Field Experiment on Labor Market Discrimination. NBER Working Paper No. 9873. July 2003 Website. February 2010. http://papers.nber.org/papers/w9873

Blank, Rebecca M., Dabady, Marilyn and Citro, Constance F., Editors Measuring Racial Discrimination: Panel on Methods for Assessing Discrimination National Research Council of the National Academies. The National Academies Press, 2004. Website. February 2010. http://books.nap.edu/catalog.php?record_id=10887

Dalton, Harlon., Racial Healing: Confronting the Fear Between Blacks and Whites. 1995

Davis, Sammy, Jr. Why Me? with Jane and Burt Boyar 1989

Delphin, Renee. Coloring Outside the Lines. The Undergraduate Magazzine about Race and Ethnicity at Yale, Simon Rodberg, Editor in Chief, November

Ford, Clyde W., We Can All Get Along: 50 Steps You Can take to Help End Racism. 1972

Gibson, Campbell and Jung, Kay. U. S. Census Bureau Historical Census Statistics on Population Totals By Race, 1790 to 1990, and By Hispanic Origin, 1970 to 1990, For The United States, Regions, Divisions, and States. Working Paper Series No. 56. n.p., September 2002. Website. February 2010. http://www.census.gov/population/www/documentation/twps0056/twps0056.html

Hacker, Andrew. Two Nations: Black and White, Separate, Hostile, Unequal 1992

Johnson, Lyndon B. Equal employment opportunity. Executive Order 11246 of September 24, 1965. Website. February 2010. http://www.archives.gov/federal-register/codification/executive-order/11246.html

Lorde, Audre. Sister Outsider. 2007. Crossing Press

Material Safty Data Sheet, printed from http://www.certified-lye.com/

Omi, Michael and Howard Winant, Racial Formation in the United States: From the 1960s to the 1980s (NY: Routledge, 1986/1989). Website February 2010. http://aad.english.ucsb.edu/docs/Omi-Winant.html

Race- The Power of an Illusion. PBS, n.d. Website. February 2010. http://www.pbs.org/race/000_General/000_00-Home.htm

Reidy, Chris and Neuwahl, Janette. Legislature cotes to repeal 1675 Hub ban on Indians: Law hurt city's bid to host convention. The Boston Globe., 20 May 2005. Website. February 2010 http://www.boston.com/business/globe/articles/2005/05/20/legislature_votes_to_repeal_1675_hub_ban_on_indians/

Trillin, Calvin American Chronicles:Black or White. The New Yorker., 14 April 1986. Website Website. February 2010 http://archives.newyorker.com/?i=1986-04-14#folio=CV1

West, Cornel. West Restoring Hope: Conversations on the Future of Black America edited by Kelvin S. Sealy. 1997

What's in a name?. MIT News. January 24, 2003 . Website. February 2010. http://web.mit.edu/newsoffice/2003/resume.html

Wise, Tim. Is Sisterhood Conditional?: White Women and the Rollback of Affirmative Action. National Women's Studies Association Journal, Fall 1998. Website. February 2010.

Zezima, Katie. Banned in Boston: American Indians, but Only for 329 Years. The New York Times. 25 November 2004. Website. February 2010. http://www.nytimes.com/2004/11/25/national/25indian.html

SCHOOLS

If you have been inspired or agitated by the stories in Speak Up! and wish to take action at your school, the following is a partial list of school contacts. If you don't see your school listed, please check our website for an updated list.

Beaver Country Day School
Robert Principe
Hiatt Center
Director of Educational Leadership
(617) 738-2709
rprincipe@bcdschool.org

The Berkshire School
Kate Garbutt
Math Teacher, SAT Tutor
(413) 229-8511 ext. 1107
kgarbutt@berkshireschool.org

Boston University Academy
Maureen Hurley
Director of Summer Programs and
Coordinator of Student Life and
Advising
(617) 353-9000
maureen_hurley@buacademcy.org

Brewster Academy
Jaime Laurent
Director of Residence Life
(603) 569-7484
jamie_laurent@brewsteracademy.org

Brimmer and May
Runeko Lovell
Diversity Director
(617) 278-2324
rlovell@brimmer.org

Brooks School
Richard Espinal
Associate Director of Admission
Director of Student of Color
(978) 725-6291
respinal@brooksschool.org

Buckingham Brown and Nichols
Ross Clark
Academic Dean
(617) 800-2220
ross_clark@bbns.org

Buxton School
C. William Bennet
Co-Director
(413) 458-3919
BBennett@BuxtonSchool.org

The Cambridge School of Weston
Judith Ellen
Associate Director of Admissions
Diversity Action Group
(781) 642-8652
jellen@csw.org

Commonwealth School
Lihuan Lai
Director of Diversity
Associate director of Admissions
(617) 266-7525
llai@commschool.org

Concord Academy
David Rost
Dean of Students and Community Life
(978) 402-2275
david_rost@concordacademy.org

Dana Hall School
Jessica Keimowitz
Director of the Upper School
(781) 235-3010 ext. 2515
jessica.keimowitz@danahall.org

Deerfield Academy
Ayodeji Perrin
College Advisor/ Asst Director of
Multicultural Affairs
(413) 774-1493
aperrin@deerfield.edu

The Fenn School
Tete Cobblah
Director of Diversity
(978) 318-3506
tcobblah@fenn.org

Kimball Union Academy
Sandy Ouellette
Assistant Director, Health Services/
Chair of the Diversity Committee
(603) 469-2055
souellette@kua.org

Lawrence Academy
Wonjen C. Bagley
Coordinator of Diversity Initiatives
(978) 448-1581
wbagley@lacademy.edu

Lincoln School
Lynn C. Varadian
Dean Of Students
(401) 331-9696 ext. 3104
lvaradian@lincolnschool.org

Will Shotwell
Director
Center for Peace Equity and Justice
through Service
(401) 331-9696 ext. 4053
wshotwell@lincolnschool.org

Thierry Gustave
Teacher, World Languages
(401) 331-9696 ext. 4030
tgustave@lincolnschool.org

Teryl Sweeney
Director of Information Services
Middle School Administrative
Assistant
(401) 331-9696 ext. 3112
tsweeney@lincolnschool.org

Anita Thompson
Department Head and Teacher,
Visual Arts
(401) 331-9696 ext. 4049
athompson@lincolnschool.org

SCHOOLS

The Meadowbrook School
Alison Graham
Director of Diversity
Physical Education Teacher
(781) 894-1193 ext. 206
AGraham@meadowbrook-ma.org

Middlesex School
Brian Smith
Assistant Dean of Students/ Director
of Diversity; History
(978) 402-1466
basmith@mxschool.edu

Millbrook School
Anthony McKinley
English Department/Diversity
Coordinator
(845) 677-8261 x114
amckinley@millbrook.org

Milton Academy
Heather Flewelling
Director of Student
Multicultural Programs
(617) 898-2150
heather_flewelling@milton.edu

Nobles and Greenough
Steven Tejada
Director of Diversity
(781) 326-3700
steven_tejada@nobles.edu

Northfield Mount Hermon School
James J. Greenwood
Director of Multicultural Education
Associate Dean of Students
(413) 498-3252
(413) 498-3439
JGreenwood@nmhschool.org

The Park School
Alice Lucey
Head of the Upper Division
(617) 274 6052
alice_lucey@parkschool.org

The Pike School
Vanessa Hynes
Diversity Committee Chair
(978) 475-1197 ext. 6629
vhynes@pikeschool.org

The Pingree School
Trina A.Gary
Director of Multicultural Education
(978) 468-4415 ext. 205
tgary@pingree.org

The Putney School
Brian D. Cohen
Dean of Faculty/ Diversity Committee
Member
(802) 387-7328
bcohen@putneyschool.org

The Rivers School
John H. Bower
French, Middle School Select Chorus,
Director of Diversity
(339) 686-2284
j.bower@rivers.org

St. George's School
Dr. Kim W. Bullock
Director of Diversity
(401) 842-6749
kim_bullock@stgeorges.edu

St. John's Prep (Danvers)
Roberto German
Director of Multi-Cultural Affairs
(978) 774-1050
rgerman@stjohnsprep.org

Tabor Academy
Anika O.Walker-Johnson
English Instructor
Director of Multicultural
Student Affairs
(508) 748-2000 ext. 2273
Johnson@taboracademy.org

Walnut Hill School
Cathy Yun
Director of International Community
Programs
508-652-7818
CYun@walnuthillarts.org

The Winsor School
Julian Braxton
Director of Diversity
(617) 739-5519
jbraxton@winsor.edu

Worcester Academy
Rodney Glasgow
Director of Diversity and
Community Relations
(508) 754-5302 Ext. 188
rodney.glasgow@worcesteracademy.
org